TOWARDS A NEW EUROPEAN IMPETUS POST-BREXIT

TOWARDS A NEW EUROPEAN IMPETUS POST-BREXIT

A View Behind the Scenes

Rudy Aernoudt

INTERSENTIA

Cambridge – Antwerp – Chicago

Intersentia Ltd
8 Wellington Mews
Wellington Street | Cambridge
CB1 1HW | United Kingdom
Tel: +44 1223 736 170
Email: mail@intersentia.co.uk
www.intersentia.com | www.intersentia.co.uk

Distribution for the UK and Rest of the World (incl. Eastern Europe)
NBN International
1 Deltic Avenue, Rooksley
Milton Keynes MK13 8LD
United Kingdom
Tel: +44 1752 202 301 | Fax: +44 1752 202 331
Email: orders@nbninternational.com

Distribution for Europe
Lefebvre Sarrut Belgium NV
Hoogstraat 139/6
1000 Brussels
Belgium
Tel: +32 (0)2 548 07 13
Email: mail@intersentia.be

Distribution for the USA and Canada
Independent Publishers Group
Order Department
814 North Franklin Street
Chicago, IL 60610
USA
Tel: +1 800 888 4741 (toll free) | Fax: +1 312 337 5985
Email: orders@ipgbook.com

ISBN 978-1-83970-322-5
D/2023/7849/19
NUR 820

British Library Cataloguing in Publication Data. A catalogue record for this book is available from the British Library.

Men accept change
only when necessary
and they only see the need
in a crisis.

Jean Monnet
*Mémoires**

---

* 'Les hommes n'acceptent le changement que dans la nécessité et ils ne voient la nécessité que dans la crise': J. Monnet, *Mémoires*, Livre de poche, 2007.

FOREWORD BY COLIN MASON

This is an ambitious book. The premise is that there is a need to modernise the appeal of Europe by developing a new narrative that (re)connects Europe's citizens – its stakeholders – to the idea of Europe and specifically one that engages Generation Z. Rudy Aernoudt is eminently qualified to offer a new narrative. He has worked almost all of his professional career in European Union Institutions – in European advisory bodies, the European Council and the European Commission. His roles have included cabinet director at European level, Special Counsellor to the European Council President and chief economist. He has also held positions as Head of Cabinet in Belgium, at federal, Flemish and Walloon level. He has significant policy achievements. He designed and implemented the Joint European Ventures (JEV) programme to stimulate European companies to set up joint ventures with companies from other European countries. He co-founded the European Business Angel Network (EBAN) and he conceived the ESCALAR (European Scale-up Action for Risk Capital) that will double the capacity of the venture capital funds to support companies at their scale-up stage. Our paths crossed in the late 1990s when EBAN was being conceived and established, and we have remained in contact, albeit sporadically, since then.

Aernoudt starts by tracking the deepening integration of Europe. The European Union was created in 1957 when the Treaty of Rome was signed, initially as an economic union comprising six Member States, expanding to 28 members (following Brexit it now has 27 members), with several states seeking membership. Over this time, Europe has evolved from its origins as an economic union. The process of economic integration has deepened, culminating in the Single Market which, in turn, paved the way for the European Monetary Union, with the Treaty of Lisbon creating a coherent set of decision-making procedures. This has resulted in the acquisition of increasingly new competences moving into non-economic fields as laws have been translated into national legislation. Aernoudt highlights the increasingly complex interplay between the European Council and the European Parliament and the exponential growth of regulations and directives, much of which relates to the internal market, complicating the daily lives of ordinary citizens. The cumulative effect has been to create what he calls a 'citizen gap' that is reflected in low voter turnout in EU elections and expressing aversion to the European project whenever they have had the opportunity, specifically voting in referendums in various countries over the years against constitutional treaties. Brexit is the most recent and dramatic illustration of citizen disenchantment with Europe.

Aernoudt defends the European project, arguing that it is often used as a scapegoat, particularly by populist movements whose narrative is that 'everything would be better without Europe'. He also observes the hypocrisy of opponents of Europe who nevertheless claim their seats in the European Parliament and its committees, along with the generous remuneration. Nevertheless, he is fully aware of Europe's weaknesses that have led this situation, highlighting the inflation of bureaucracy with its consequent paralysing effect on activity, its 'legislative zeal' that has created what many regard as the over-regulation of the daily lives of citizens (which is often vocalised as 'interference' in the affairs of Member States) and specifically 'the urge to prohibit', decision-making processes that are opaque, and a democratic deficiency that has resulted from the shift from unanimity to qualified majority voting (although unanimity continues in some domains). He also criticises the European Parliament for becoming a bureaucracy in its own right and its advisory committees, specifically their procedures and relationships between officials and elected members, leading him to question whether they add value.

So, how should Europe proceed? Answering this question forms the core of the book. Aernoudt identifies several options. He makes the case for a pragmatic approach that involves going back to its core values – further developing the internal market, aligning economic policy more closely with monetary policy and developing a social policy worthy of its name – to focus on those areas where it can make tangible improvements to the quality of life of its citizens. This requires a 'mean and lean structure' that involves (i) the reduction of bureaucracy, notably by cutting back on the number of Commissioners and the size of its other institutions and the European Parliament; (ii) a reduction in the number of officials (who, he notes, are mostly appointed for life); (iii) scaling back on activity, with involvement limited to where there is a clear European dimension and involving several countries; (iv) curbing its desire to harmonize; and (v) stop seeking to compete with the United States.

Based on these principles, he develops twelve priorities for action at a European level that will make a difference to its citizens that they will experience in their everyday lives: (i) Erasmus student mobility programmes to promote multilingualism and polycultures (and extend this to young entrepreneurs); (ii) environmental and climate programmes; (iii) industry policy focused on manufacturing to reverse the loss of jobs and actively seeking to reshore them; (iv) developing space travel – which encompasses telecoms, navigation and observation – to achieve strategic autonomy from the United States and China; (v) creating entrepreneurial mindsets and a supportive environment to stimulate entrepreneurial activity; (vi) innovation policy, focusing on the scale-up funding gap; (vii) continuing to develop the internal market – which is still a work in progress – with reforms; (viii) Euro and monetary policy which brings all non-Euro countries into the Euro; (ix) the pursuit of Keynesian economic policy along the lines of the COVID-19 recovery fund; (x) employability strategies with social support that provide work for all; (xi) social and regional policy to reduce social and regional disparities; and (xii) foreign policy that restricts external economic relationships to countries that respect European values and reverses strategic dependency on other countries for key raw materials, inputs and technologies.

Aernoudt is optimistic that his agenda can be achieved. First, he suggests that Brexit has provided a fresh impetus for a new Europe. It has prompted Eurocrats to ask: 'what have we done wrong?' It has removed the British attitude of reluctance to change that was often an excuse that other countries used to hide behind. It has also made the remaining 27 countries more European. Second, crises act as accelerators of the European integration process. Financing through European loans would never have been possible without the COVID-19 crisis. The Ukraine crisis has accelerated energy transition. Climate change is driving societal and economic change. The challenge that Aernoudt emphasizes at various point in the book is to ensure that this impetus to create a new Europe is not lost.

Colin Mason
Professor of Entrepreneurship
Adam Smith Business School, University of Glasgow, Scotland, UK

FOREWORD BY HENRI MALOSSE

The Twelve Works of Rudy Aernoudt

Books about Europe appear every week, but few are written by someone who is currently experiencing the European institutions from within. Rudy was my chief of staff during my presidency of the European Economic and Social Committee. He was Special Adviser to the Presidency of the European Council and held various positions at the European Commission. And in all of these functions, he acted more as an entrepreneur than as a civil servant.

Moreover, Rudy also knows Europe from the point of view of the Member States, as well as from that of the regions. He was in fact chief of staff in his own country, Belgium, at both regional and federal level. He was thus private secretary on the three levels, a unique achievement worthy of an entry in the Guinness Book of Records.

These multiple experiences are reflected in his book. We feel his passion for Europe. But also, we feel the desire for Europe to move forward. Instead of complaining about the crises that Europe is going through and has been through, the author argues that Europe is able to overcome these crises, and more importantly, to take advantage of them to progress and develop. He therefore calls for the COVID crisis not to be wasted, but to be used as a lever for the further integration of Europe.

However, the author is not a blind 'Euro-lover' who would like everything to be done at European level. He points out the danger, as also shown by Max Weber, that the formalism of bureaucracy can lead to cumbersome and rigid administrative procedures, even to a monopolization of power in favour of the bureaucrats' interests. Bureaucracy is indeed a system that provokes resistance to change, a system that revolves around itself and loses its link with the outside world. The bubble of the Schuman roundabout, as the author calls it, is one of the main issues explaining the disassociation with the European citizen.

But this bureaucratic mechanism failed to extinguish the flame of the European dream for the author, a passion that keeps him looking at solutions instead of problems. This is what I admire most about him: a pragmatic spirit coupled with an unrelenting optimism.

And since the author uses anecdotes in his book, allow me to do the same. In our cabinet, employees had to put a euro in 'the pot' every time they used the word 'problem'. The pot was big enough to host drinks every Friday night. But most importantly, it brought with it a 'solution-driven attitude', as the English say (now unfortunately ex-members of the EU).

In my book *Le crépuscule des Bureaucrates*, freely translated as *The eve of the Bureaucrats*, to which the author also refers, I have already pointed out the risk of the end of European construction as a result of technocracy. Both Rudy and I deplore the yawning gulf between Europe and its citizens. Yes, there are still Eurocrats who 'have European stars in their eyes' and many Eurocrats had tears in their eyes when Brexit was announced; but that does not represent the majority.

Rudy Aernoudt, a convinced European, alumnus of the College of Europe, is just as passionate about Europe as I am. In the name of a Europe of the citizens, he makes an inimitable plea for a responsible and efficient bureaucracy at the service of the citizen.

This should prompt the Eurocrat not to become a lackey of the system, incapable of making moral judgments. 'The Banality of Evil', as Hannah Arendt called it, referring to the 'model official' Adolf Eichman, who largely achieved his goals without condemning the ethical consequences of his actions. 'He was not guilty, not mean, but rather, mediocre', concluded Hannah Arendt. The author, who is not only an economist but also a philosopher, argues for a responsible bureaucracy in which ethics is the common thread in every action. There is only one key question the author asks, referring to the book *The Stranger* by Camus: 'does what we do at European level improve the quality of life for citizens or not?'

On the basis of this, the author argues that Europe should stop meddling in everything and focus clearly on things where it can make a difference to the well-being of its citizens. He maps out the most important projects, such as the internal market launched by Jacques Delors and which is still not completed. He calls them the twelve labours of Hercules.

I have always appreciated the author for his positive and decisive attitude, laced with humour and a cheerful, direct style that we find very clearly in this educational and also humorous book. By avoiding Euro-jargon, the book reads extremely smoothly for a subject that is essentially very important for all of our futures.

The author, who likes to refer to mythology, would certainly say that the Greek god Kairos, the god of the right time, stands by him. Indeed, never has the European Union, destabilized by Brexit, been so fragile, torn between the different interests of North and South, together with the tensions with Russia, meaning that the Cold War and wars in general are on our doorstep.

I encourage you to read this book. It is aimed both at politicians looking for a vision, and at citizens who want to understand and influence their own future. The gap between citizens and the European Union today is so profound that it will not be bridged without pragmatism and the author's twelve Works. So, let's all be like him, as Jean Monnet would say: 'neither optimist nor pessimist, but determined'.

Henri Malosse
President of the Jean Monnet Foundation
Former President of the European Economic and Social Committee

PREFACE

Founded in its current form in 1957, Europe has reached retirement age. However, it does not appear that Europe can rest on its laurels. In referendums, citizens systematically speak out against it. Populist movements in France and the Netherlands, among others, oppose Europe and are calling for the reintroduction of their national currencies. For the first time in the history of the European Union, a member has even chosen to leave the club. And during the post-Brexit negotiations, the COVID-19 crisis hit, which, like any crisis, gave rise to nationalist reflexes. How did it come to this? How can such a beautiful project – at least on paper – suffer such a significant blow? And what is next?

Europe is a phoenix in this regard. The deeper the crisis, the more is possible. The institutional crisis led to the single market project, the banking crisis led to the banking union, the COVID-19 crisis made possible what had never happened before – the issuance of European bonds – and the Ukraine crisis accelerated the energy transition. It is as if Europe can only arise and evolve as a result of crises.

Why write another book about Europe? A new book on Europe is published almost every week, for or against Europe. Everyone has an opinion about how to proceed and European experts are mushrooming. Most of these experts only know Europe from other books and write a new book about it that is often a mosaic of existing texts. Intertextuality, as the French philosopher Julia Kristeva calls it. We could call it 'cut and paste' culture today.

I therefore felt it was my responsibility to write about Europe based on my professional experience within the European institutions. A vision of someone who has experienced and lived Europe, as a European in daily life, but also from within, from the Brussels Eurocrat bubble. This explains the title of this book: *Towards a New European Impetus Post-Brexit: A View Behind the Scenes.*

My triple position as head of cabinet in Belgium, at federal, Flemish and Walloon level, was rather an interlude in my life. After all, I have worked almost my entire professional life for Europe. I have worked in the European advisory bodies, the European Council and the European

Commission and attended the sessions of the European Parliament in Strasbourg countless times. I was cabinet director at European level, special counsellor to the European Council President, chief economist and more of those lofty titles.

So I am, as it is called in the Euro-jargon, a Eurocrat. For many, this is a kind of swear word associated with an overpaid and underworked caste. Incidentally, I was born a few years after the creation of the European Union and will therefore soon be ending my European professional career. I therefore regard this book as the will of a Eurocrat, a will in the sense of 'testimony', the writing of a privileged witness. It will therefore start with a critical analysis of Europe based on my many years of experience in various European institutions. On the basis of my analysis and my experience, I want to then outline some guidelines for the Europe of the future.

In a previous book, *Vlaanderen-Wallonië, je t'aime, moi non plus [Flanders, Wallonia, I love you, I don't care]*, I focused on the relationship between Flemings and Walloons, a love–hate relationship. I added an analysis about their bastard child in *Brussels, Enfant Mal aimé [Brussels, the unloved child]*. And in *Coronavirus: Electroshock voor België [Coronavirus: Electroshock for Belgium]*, I set out my vision on the future of Belgium and on the question of what policy is desperately needed. But for me there is no future for Flanders, Wallonia, Brussels or Belgium outside Europe. No future for France or Paris, Great Britain or London, the Netherlands or Amsterdam, to name a few, outside Europe. Europe is and remains the cradle of our culture, our civilization and our economy. At the end of my life, I do not want to see Europe deteriorate further and end up in economic dementia. I do not want Europe to be the continent where the proverbial sun sets. From this perspective, I deeply regret Brexit and hope that one day Great Britain, as a whole, will re-join the European Union. It will take at least a generation, but never say never.

Does that mean that everything is running perfectly in Europe? No, not at all. Europe has lost touch with its grandchildren. The slogan 'no more war' only appeals to contemporaries and cannot be a permanent legitimacy for Europe, even if the Ukraine crisis shows that 'no more war' is never an '*acquis*'. But the future of Europe can only be positive if Europe represents an added value for all its citizens and not for the 'happy few'. Europe can only have a future if it also has a story that appeals to the next generation. That is the big challenge: what is the narrative – as Eurocrats call it – of Europe today? How does Europe make sure that its citizens have a better life because of it? How can we respond to populists who argue that everything would be better without Europe?

In the first chapter of this book, I describe how Europe works. This is not just another pedagogical book or a description of the institutions. For this you can go to various websites or consult the various brochures from and about Europe, which are free of charge. No, I want to give you a look behind the scenes. I think this is the best way to understand Europe and its institutions. In the first chapter, I summarize the phenomena that have resulted in Europe finding itself in turbulent waters. This analysis makes it possible in the second chapter to discuss the possible solutions that present themselves for Europe. In the third and fourth chapters, I discuss my vision of what Europe could look like in concrete terms in the future and what actions – I call them the Twelve Labours of Hercules – Europe should take in this regard. These actions are how Europe could succeed in really improving the quality of life of European citizens. Because, as the Japanese saying goes, action without vision is a nightmare.

My aim is to write about Europe with as little Eurocrat jargon as possible. I hope to have succeeded in this objective. I thank Patrick Power, with whom I had long discussions on Brexit and who was so kind, as a native speaker, to fine-tune my translation. In order to present things very concretely, I have included examples in twelve boxes in the text. Reactions and comments are, as always, welcome at raernoudt@gmail.com.

Enjoy reading!

CONTENTS

CHAPTER 1

EUROPE: FROM DREAM TO ACTION

between dream and deed
stand in the way laws
and practical objections

'Marriage'
Willem Elsschot[1]

The founding fathers of Europe can look back with satisfaction. Few believed in Schuman and Monnet's plan. Getting the legendary warriors around the table or, more importantly, bringing their interests together in one organization seemed like a mission impossible. And yet it worked. Gone are the days when Germany and France were on the warpath every 20 or 30 years. And that is what it was all about in the end.

But does that success still appeal to young people? For Generation Z, war is something out of history books or in regions far away from Europe. Even the Ukraine conflict has not changed that mindset. The slogan 'no more war' sounds hollow. Former combatants and ex-prisoners of concentration camps who can bring history to life with their testimonies are almost non-existent. The books by Anne Frank, Primo Levi or Jorge Semprún are stories from the past, from the old days. Moving, yes, but long gone. Cyberattacks and hackers appeal more to the imagination than trenches.

And would the founding fathers be happy to see the army of Eurocrats, empty plenary sessions and the travelling theatre from Brussels to

---

1 Willem Elsschot is one of the best-known and most important Flemish authors of the twentieth century. 'Marriage', where a man watches his aging wife in horror, is his most famous poem.

Strasbourg? Would the founding fathers be happy if they were to see that Europe is absent in areas of paramount importance for citizens, such as migration policy? Would they be happy if they found that a coordinated approach to border controls in the fight against COVID-19 proved impossible? Would they be happy to see that the British people expressed their wish to leave the Union?

To answer these questions, we briefly look at the basic idea of Europe and analyse how this beautiful idea has developed, resulting in a Europe that has lost its connection with Europeans. In an analogy to Willem Elsschot's marriage, we can say that for Europe, too, laws stand between dream and deed and practical objections arise. The marriage between Europe and its citizens, like most marriages, is therefore a bumpy road.

1. FROM GENESIS TO BREXIT

1.1. NO MORE WAR

23 June 2016: thunderclap from a clear sky. In a referendum, 51% of Britons are in favour of Brexit. The defeat is great for many thinking Europeans. How did it come to this? For the first time I see in the eyes of many fellow Eurocrats disbelief and at the same time the big question: what have we done wrong? Others – especially the British – think about their own fate. Will we be able to stay? We are no longer British, but rather European diplomats. Many undertook the administrative procedures to take up Belgian nationality. However, since they did not pay income tax in Belgium, it did not seem so easy: and our pensions, who will pay for them now? The legendary phlegmatic character of the British was nowhere to be found. Perhaps after all those years in Brussels they had become Europeanized Britons. Human, all too human, I thought to myself, referring to one of my favourite books by Friedrich Nietzsche.

The trade unions – yes, they also exist in European institutions – jumped into the breach and promised to do everything necessary to safeguard the acquired rights – their universal buzzword. The real drama, the fact that the European project was dealt a huge blow, faded into the background for a while. The public interest again had to give way to the individual interest. How many times had I experienced that?[2]

---

2 For the interested reader, see my book *Coronavirus: Electroshock voor België [Coronavirus: Electroshock for Belgium]*, Van Gompel & Svacina, 2020.

The British were not there when the European idea took concrete shape. Between the British and Europe, the water has always been – literally – deep, and as bad as their exit is, let us face it, it was not a founding member who left the ship. Their dream was not a political union, but a free trade zone. With the agreement that took effect on 1 January 2021, they had de facto achieved this.

1.2. GENESIS

To understand Brexit, we have to go back to the origins of the European idea. During the first half of the twentieth century, European countries tore each other apart. French and Germans fought in the name of their respective homeland, and so against one another and de facto against any thought of European cooperation. It is therefore not surprising that the aftermath of the World Wars formed the perfect conditions for a large-scale project of cooperation. No more war by bringing together strategic interests: that is how we could summarize the origin of the European project.

Europe is not alone in these aspirations. History is peppered with examples of successful and unsuccessful attempts by countries to cooperate in one way or another, and examples of such attempts can be found almost all over the world. So, it should not surprise us that we also tried this in Europe. In this sense, European history is not unique in its efforts, although perhaps in its achievements.

Efforts to get (a number of) European countries to cooperate are also not new. The history of Europe can be seen as an ever-recurring process characterized by peaceful or non-peaceful attempts at integration (but also at disintegration) and a restless search for its true identity.

The history of Europe can therefore best be described as being defined by the Greek gods Eros, god of love, and Eris, goddess of battle. The history of Europe is indeed a series of declarations of love and declarations of war. Often, they were both means of achieving the same goal, namely gaining power over persons or regions. As is the case of the individual human being, love and hate are also closely related here.

This had already started with the emergence of Europe. The child exists as soon as it has a name, as the well-known French psychoanalyst Jacques Lacan taught us.[3] If we apply this thesis to Europe, we should therefore

3 J. Lacan, *Ecrits [Writings]*, Seuil, 1966.

first probe into the origin of the name. The Greek myth about this is well known. The supreme god Zeus saw a beautiful young girl enjoying herself on the sea wall with her playmates and fell in love instantly. He took the form of a white bull and mingled with the girls. He let the girls stroke him and the young girl named Europa could not resist the temptation to sit on the bull's back. Immediately, the bull straightened up, walked into the sea and swam out into deep waters. Only when the bull had swum over the horizon, to the island of Crete, did he reveal his true identity to the girl. He took her name for the continent where he had brought her ashore.

Love and deception, abduction and rapture go hand in hand from the very beginning. So, the original scene of a declaration of love and seduction is anything but imbued with ethical principles. The three gifts, a chiastic word,[4] that Zeus offered to his beloved Europa, with whom he begat three sons, are also indicative of the inherent relationship between love and strife: the spear that never misses its target; the dog Laelaps, who never lets his prey escape; and the bronze man Talos, who makes his rounds every day on Crete to kill strangers. So far for the myth.

It should come as no surprise that Zeus then brought his beloved ashore in Crete and not, for example, in London, Paris, Berlin or Brussels (we mean this metaphorically, of course). Geographically, this can of course be explained by the fact that Zeus kidnapped Europa in Phoenicia, where her father was king. But more relevant is the fact that the centre of gravity of Europe's political power was for a long time situated with the Greeks and the Romans, i.e. in the south of Europe. It is only over time that power has shifted to the north and west. What we today call structurally poor areas are in fact the cradle of civilization of our continent. This points not only to a shift in power, but also to a change in the concept of power.

Power is today interpreted as economic power and is measured in terms of gross domestic product. The stakes of wars are no longer the 'civilized' regions, but the economically interesting areas. Wars, partly with the aim of achieving integration, thus acquired an economic connotation. From Charlemagne, to Napoleon, to Hitler, they all had in fact a process of economic integration in mind. Their aim was to rule over the economic powers in Europe. War was the means. However, the means often remained in the foreground and became an end in itself. Successive wars resulted. And even the Ukraine conflict is about territory, whereby geopolitical

4 A chiasm is the Greek letter χ, which refers to a double, opposite meaning. Just like the word 'gift', the word *pharmakon* is a chiasm because it refers to poison (death) as well as to cure (life) at the same time.

considerations – the lost power of the USSR after the disintegration of the bloc – are combined with economic considerations. One should not forget that the pro-Russian Donbas region has hidden lithium deposits with great potential.

In this respect, these various attempts differ from the one made in the aftermath of the Second World War. The aim in this latter case was not dominion, but peace; the means not war, but economic integration. Incidentally, it was a very ambitious project that was labelled by many as utopian. Some argued that apparently only a conqueror can bring about European unification.[5] The attempt did compare with earlier efforts – which used less peaceful techniques – when once again the means remained in the foreground and supplanted the original goal.

The European Community is indeed first and foremost an economic community. Although its founders and pioneers from the very beginning presented the European Community primarily as a solution aimed at curbing the war aspirations of European countries, it was immediately pragmatic. Avoiding war is not done by signing universal ethical declarations, but by separating the potential sources of conflict from national rule and entrusting them to a supranational authority. The European Community wanted to forge some new economic ties to counter future war intentions.

Strategic economic sectors therefore had to be removed from national supervision. It is precisely this strategy that has been applied to key sectors of the economy. On 9 May 1950, the day that has since been marked as a European holiday and a holiday for Eurocrats, Robert Schuman proposed the integration of the production and consumption of coal and steel through a European organization between Germany and France, which would be open to all European countries and managed by a European institution.

The post-war climate – Europe had suffered three wars in less than a hundred years – favoured such initiatives and less than a year later the European Coal and Steel Community (ECSC) was established by six countries (besides France and Germany, Italy, Belgium, the Netherlands and Luxembourg). Management was entrusted to the High Authority. At the same time, a Council of Ministers, a Court of Justice and a Parliamentary Assembly were created. These institutions, albeit in an updated version, still form the basic structure of the European Union.

---

5 See M.A.G. Van Meerhaeghe, *Museum of grootmacht. De identiteitscrisis van Europa [Museum of Superpower. Europe's Identity Crisis]*, Lannoo, 1985, p. 211.

But it did not stop at that one initiative. The early experience with the ECSC and the post-war impetus led to two new initiatives: a European Defence Community and a European Political Community. The underlying philosophy was the same: if we can reconcile defence interests and economic and political interests, then war between those countries is highly unlikely.

The Act of the European Defence Community was solemnly signed on 27 May 1952 by the six ECSC countries. However, the treaty was not ratified by the French National Assembly, which formally rejected the treaty on 30 August 1954. One of the reasons is that France thought that, given the death of Stalin in 1953, the Cold War would shortly be over. It would take 40 years before another attempt – as part of the Maastricht Treaty – was narrowly accepted by the French National Assembly and on the basis of a referendum. The concrete implementation of this part of the Maastricht Treaty is still very modest today and the Juncker Commission considered the further development of a European Defence Union to be a priority. In 2020, 66 years later, the Defence and Space (DEFIS) Directorate was established. That is how long it can take in Europe.

The failure of the defence community also meant that from then on, the European Community once again remained primarily an economic community.

The European Community project was initially developed as an extension of the ECSC to other sectors. The aim was, on the one hand, to create a general economic union and a nuclear energy union. There was no question of a political union for the time being. This led to the Treaty of Rome, which was signed in 1957 and ratified by a large majority in all parliaments. As a result, in addition to the ECSC, the European Economic Community (EEC) and the European Atomic Energy Community (Euratom) were created. The United Kingdom, which was involved in the negotiations, stood aside and set up a free trade area with six other European countries (Switzerland, Norway, Sweden, Denmark, Portugal and Austria): the European Free Trade Association (EFTA). This zone, too, is a purely economic approach which guarantees free access to the members; markets, but, in contrast to the then EEC, without imposing common external tariffs on its members. Of the founding members, only Switzerland and Norway are still EFTA members, but were joined by Lichtenstein and Iceland.

The idea of the free trade zone was re-posted by the British after Brexit as a form of cooperation with the EU-27, to which they no longer belonged. *L'histoire se répète.*

1.3. THE INTERNAL MARKET

Bearing in mind the materialist thesis of Marx and Engels, which states that solutions to economic problems are the necessary preconditions for solutions to political problems, economic success led to new attempts at political cooperation. However, these attempts invariably failed, mainly due to differences of opinion between the large and small Member States of the EEC. The solution of economic problems is a necessary, but apparently not a sufficient, condition. The process of European integration has therefore de facto become a process of economic integration. The reduction of tariff barriers was successfully completed (1958–1968) and after a paralysis of the economic integration process, mainly as a result of the unanimity rule, the second phase, namely the reduction of non-tariff barriers, was realized under the brand name Europa '92 (1985–1993).

The success of this approach can be deduced, among other things, from the increasing number of members. Five of the founding members of EFTA had meanwhile joined the European Union club. Over more than half a century – between 1958 and 2016 – the club grew from six to 28 members. We have thus almost arrived at the initial pan-European idea, as formulated a hundred years ago by Richard Coudenhove-Kalergi, the forgotten father of the European Union in 1923, to arrive at a European bloc from the Urals to Gibraltar.[6] According to him, this was the only solution to prevent the expansion of Bolshevism into Europe and the Americanization of Europe.[7]

After all, the single market was not only the breeding ground for economic cooperation between European citizens and European companies, but also became the nucleus for political cooperation. We might argue that the economy indeed determines politics, and not the other way around. The single market paved the way for a new economic project: the European monetary union. This project, which had been attempted on several occasions and failed each time, suddenly became possible. 'One market, one currency,' the European leaders shouted in unison. But countries like the United Kingdom and Denmark were reluctant to surrender their currency. Of the 28 countries, only nineteen belong to the European monetary union. This made European integration at different speeds a reality.

---

6 R. Coudenhove-Kalergi, *Pan-Europa*, orig. 1923 Cent Mille Millards, 2019.

7 P. Gerbet, *La construction de l'Europe [The Building of Europe]*, Imprimerie Nationale, 1999, p. 33.

1.4. THE BRUSSELS OCTOPUS

But precisely because of this progress, the interference of Europe in the daily life of Europeans became more tangible. Donor countries also felt that the costs were too high. Europe became too bureaucratic and too expensive. 'I want my money back,' shouted former UK Prime Minister Margaret Thatcher at the opening of the College of Europe in 1985. As a former student, I sat in the front row and, not knowing any better, applauded because I also thought that the creeping bureaucratization of Europe was detrimental to the European idea. Little did I know then that this British Euroscepticism would lead to Brexit 30 years later. Indeed, after years of expansion, the European project suddenly made a U-turn, which could have been the prelude to a downward spiral. This process would also bear the seeds of a disintegration, which culminated with Brexit. For the first time in history, a member decided to leave the club. This was so improbable that nothing was foreseen in the treaties for that scenario. It was only eighteen months after the referendum, on 25 November 2018, that the United Kingdom and the EU were able to reach a difficult understanding on the 500-page divorce agreement, which was only approved by the British Parliament after new elections in the United Kingdom in January 2020. 'Get Brexit done' was the political slogan of the newly elected Prime Minister Boris Johnson. Incidentally, this famous Brexiteer had frequently argued before that Britain benefits from being in the EU to influence its decisions. Or, as he stated in his own words in an interview with the German magazine *Der Spiegel*: 'We can't leave Europe. We're part of the European Continent. What is the English Channel? It's a primeval river that got slightly too big.'[8]

Meanwhile, according to polls, a majority of Britons, especially the younger generation, were now against Brexit. In fact, the younger generation had never even been in favour of Brexit. The older generation decided on the future of the country, usurping in this way the younger generation's right to decide on their European future. Brexit would bring in £350 million a week to be used to fund the National Health Service (NHS), the unsubstantiated demagoguery said. The fact that economic studies, in particular those of the UK Planning Bureau, suggested that the cost of Brexit could be estimated at £80 billion a year, or £1,540 million a week,

---

8 T. Hüetlin and C. Scheuermann, 'We Can't Leave Europe, We're Part of the Continent', *Spiegel International*, 12.08.2015, https://www.spiegel.de/international/europe/spiegel-interview-with-london-mayor-boris-johnson-a-1047789.html.

underlined the power of the demagoguery against truth.[9] The British community even remained indifferent when, as early as the day after the referendum, the Brexiteers stated that their calculations were unfounded.

Indeed, the straw that broke the camel's back was not monetary in nature, but legal. The European Economic Community (EEC) was renamed the European Community (EC) by the Maastricht Treaty. This points to the will to grant competence to the European institutions in non-economic areas as well. The most striking example of this is that European citizens' rights are accorded regardless of their economic situation. Thus, the freedom of circulation for persons is no longer conditional on the exercise of some economic activity in the host country. Talos, the bronze man, could now focus on non-Europeans who lived on the European continent. However, the refugee crisis meant that many non-economic migrants went to European countries. The failure of a European policy on the matter was probably one of the main reasons why the British abandoned Europe. Not Brussels but London had to determine refugee policy, Nigel Farage, leader of the UK Independence Party (UKIP), proclaimed, while he was on the payroll of the European Parliament. He was supported in this by gigantic posters with photos of queuing migrants, adorning London double-decker buses. Propaganda and demagoguery are of all times. Indeed, ideological polarization immediately eliminates the very possibility of a nuanced position, stated the well-known French journalist Jean Birnbaum, referring to Albert Camus, who summarized this attitude so well by saying that we are suffocating among people who are absolutely right.[10]

Europe has acquired increasingly more competences. The powers of the European institutions in research and development, environment and cohesion have been expanded. New competences have also been granted in areas where the European institutions traditionally had no competence, notably in education, youth, culture and health. The competence here mainly encompasses a policy of encouragement and not so much a policy of harmonization. In addition, the European institutions were given competence in the field of consumer protection and social policy, two competences that were considerably expanded with the Treaty of Amsterdam and to which employment policy would also be added. After 40 years, the European Economic Community was finally able to leave

---

9 The Office for Budget Responsibility that made the calculations in 2016 stated five years later that their estimates were accurate and that the cost of Brexit exceeded twice the cost of the COVID-19 crisis: Office for Budget Responsibility, *Economic and Fiscal Outlook*, October 2021.

10 J. Birnbaum, *Le courage de la nuance [The Courage of Nuance]*, Seuil, 2022.

its economic cocoon. In this way, the European Community would move ever more into the field of the non-economic, and Europe would become involved in many areas that determine our daily lives. This gave rise to the perception that 'everything' was decided in Brussels. 'We want our country back' was the slogan of the British Brexit propaganda.

1.5. COMPLEXITY TRIUMPHS

This propaganda was, of course, facilitated by the hyper-complexity of the European legal framework. The European Community was embedded in the European Union by the Maastricht Treaty, which, in addition to the European Community (first pillar), also included foreign and security policy (second pillar), and justice and internal affairs (third pillar). However, foreign policy, security policy, justice and internal affairs were not integrated into Community functioning. This means that decisions in these areas are not taken through the Community method, but between heads of government. The division between the Community method and the intergovernmental approach implied legally that there were two consolidated versions of the treaties.

On the one hand, there was the Treaty on European Union. This treaty, referred to as TEU, discusses the three pillars of the European Union mentioned above. Decisions on common and security policies are taken by the Council. In other words, decisions are taken by governments without recourse to the Community's institutional apparatus. That is why we speak of the intergovernmental method.

On the other hand, there was the Treaty establishing the European Community, as drafted in Rome and successively amended, inter alia, by the Act of Unity, Maastricht, Amsterdam and Nice. This treaty, called TEC for short, discusses the various policy areas of the European Community and also of the various institutions (Commission, Council, Parliament) and the way in which they take decisions together.

Since the two treaties and the various amendments and additions made the whole thing quite opaque, the Nice Summit called for the treaties to be simplified so that they would be clearer and easier to understand, without however changing their content.[11] In other words, it was a call for a simple

---

11 Declaration on the Future of the Union, incorporated as Annex IV to the Nice Conclusions, December 2000.

and transparent 'constitution' for Europe. The coexistence of the two methods and the two treaties also led to confusion as to the powers of the national parliaments. That had to be clarified as well. And above all, how can you communicate easily to citizens about something so inaccessible and incomprehensible? How can you use such complex 'weapons' to fight demagoguery and fake news?

To simplify things, an attempt was made to make a constitution for Europe. Presenting a draft constitution to the population was of course not smart. Who reads a constitution? French and Dutch voters rejected the constitution in 2005, but four years later a text that was, according to the British think tank Open Europe, 96% similar was approved. The Lisbon Treaty was a cosmetic adjustment to the rejected constitution, said Valéry Giscard d'Estaing, chair of the working group that wrote the constitution. But this time there was no referendum, with the exception of Ireland. And yes, Ireland rejected the treaty, but still accepted it in a second referendum so as not to become isolated.

The Lisbon Treaty replaced the rejected European constitution, although the differences were mainly external. The aim was to complete the process initiated by the Treaty of Amsterdam and the Treaty of Nice with a view to enhancing the effectiveness and democratic legitimacy of the Union and making its action more coherent The main changes enshrined in the Treaty of Lisbon concerned the abolition of the European pillar structure, the increased importance of qualified majority voting in the European Council, a greater role for the European Parliament, and the introduction of a President of the European Council and the High Representative for Foreign Affairs.

The Charter of Fundamental Rights of the European Union also became legally binding. The Treaty of Lisbon merged the various procedures applicable to each pillar into one coherent set of decision-making procedures. This means that there are no separate decision-making procedures for the three policy areas. Decision-making in foreign and security policy, however, is generally still taken by the European Council on the basis of unanimity.

1.6. THE CLUB IS GROWING

As the Treaty of Rome provided only for the rule of unanimity, this meant that only the initial project of the abolition of tariff barriers could be realized. Once this momentum was over, nothing further took place in terms of further integration until the Unity Act came into force. It is true that countries left EFTA to join the European Community. This happened for the first time in 1973, when the United Kingdom, the initiator of EFTA, joined the Community, together with Ireland and Denmark. About ten years later, Greece became a member, and then Spain and Portugal (an ex-EFTA member as well) joined in 1986. However, this broadening was not accompanied by a deepening of the Community.

It was only after the ratification of the Unity Act that deepening took place. The enlargement process was therefore temporarily halted in order to allow the Member States to adjust to the internal market and prepare for the single currency. The unification of Germany provided a special exception to that rule, as five new regions, belonging to a single Member State, joined the Community here (technically we are talking about the FNL, the *fünf neue Länder*). After the advent of the single market and the ratification of the Maastricht Treaty, Austria, Sweden (both ex-EFTA members) and Finland were also able to join the Community. The Norwegians spoke out against membership for the second time in a referendum and became de facto the leader of the remaining EFTA. The Norwegian Eurocrats already recruited to prepare for accession remained in the Commission as a relic of abandoned accession.

The Treaty of Nice and the Treaty of Lisbon paved the way for the accession of countries from Central and Eastern Europe. Broadening and deepening would go hand in hand. The '*acquis communautaire*' became increasingly more extensive for candidate countries, and the entry ticket to the European Union consequently became more expensive. But the European Union nevertheless succeeded in becoming an integrated region of 28 countries, mainly because of the integration of the Central and Eastern European countries that were liberated from the Russian and Communist yoke.

The door was left ajar for further expansion. A dozen new candidates, mainly Balkan countries after the Balkan War, presented themselves. Some, such as Montenegro and Kosovo, adopted the euro as their official currency, even though they did not belong to the European Union, let alone the eurozone. Macedonia was even willing to change its name to North Macedonia to escape the veto of neighbouring Greece. Albania and Serbia, to name but a few, all wanted to join the club and took the necessary steps to get the accession process going. And the Ukrainians indicated at Maidan Nezalezhnosti a request for membership but were blocked by their own leaders. Can one imagine what would have happened if, in 2014, negotiations with Ukraine had commenced? Would there have been a Ukraine conflict?

Some already dreamed out loud of a Europe with more than 40 members. The appeal of Europe was great. In addition, the after-effects of the financial crisis had largely been controlled. European banks, thanks in part to the banking union and the Basel regulations, which were eagerly translated into European directives and regulations, were again solid.[12] The eurozone was rescued and Member States gradually reduced their debts. The populist right could not have lived up to the promise of the polls in countries such as France and the Netherlands. Unemployment fell in most countries. Financial markets rose eleven years in a row. All the lights were green.

Eurocrats breathed a sigh of relief. And then came Brexit. And if that was not enough COVID-19 plunged the world into a deep recession and Europe suffered heavily. But as one of the founding fathers of Europe put it, people are only prepared to accept change in crisis situations. And changes for Europe were urgently needed anyway. After 'the Commission of the last chance', as announced by former Commission President Jean-Claude Juncker when he took office, another Commission took office, finally headed by a woman. Would a new impetus still be possible?

2. THE FLOOD OF LAW

If you destroy a free market,
you create a black market.
If you make 10,000 regulations,
you destroy all respect for the law.

Winston Churchill
Speech in the House of Commons
3 February 1949

In addition to the complexity, Europe made the mistake of wanting to get involved with just about everything, which indeed led to the metaphorical 10,000 regulations Churchill refers to. It is estimated that 80–85% of

[12] A directive is only binding as to its result and leaves Member States free in terms of the legal transposition into national law; a regulation is immediately applicable in all Member States. On the transposition of the Basel regulations into European legislation, I refer to my book *Financial Management in Practice*, 2nd edn, Intersentia, 2019.

national and regional legislation is simply a translation – technically called transposition – of European rules. Indeed, where the European story began with strategic sectors, its influence gradually extended to all areas that shape the lives of Europeans. In its legislative zeal, Europe regulated the length of cucumbers, the production processes of cheeses, the cod desalination technique, the orientation of children's slides and so on. Although each of these regulations is based on the noblest of intentions and is substantiated by all kinds of committees, the whole comes across as a cluttered patchwork of rules in which the citizen gets lost. The 'interference' of Europe is therefore perceived as an interference in national and regional politics. Citizens cannot make sense of the labyrinth and Europe is the scapegoat.

This flood of law is often perceived as a Brussels octopus that interferes with everything. As a Latvian student I met on one of my many missions vigorously summarized it: 'For us nothing changed; before it was Moscow, now it's Brussels.' That perception, which is not at all in line with Europe's intention – but as the German philosopher Emmanuel Kant put it, perception is reality – is often the reason why citizens turn away from the European idea. Before we explain a few poignant examples by way of illustration, how does such European law come about?

2.1. THE GOLDEN TRIANGLE

The European institutions were developed on the French model, with a Commission (right of initiative), a Council (power of decision) and a Parliament (power of co-decision). The relationship within this decision triangle evolved naturally due to the change in the voting procedure. For example, the Parliament, originally an advisory body, gained in importance, much to the frustration of the European Economic and Social Committee, which remained an advisory body. In addition to that committee, a second committee was set up to give an advisory voice as the mouthpiece of the regions: the Committee of the Regions. There is also a Court of Audit and a Court of Justice of the European Union.

Legislative proposals come from the Commission. The Commission, which therefore has the right of initiative, is a gigantic machine that makes proposals and also monitors implementation. Its proposals are discussed simultaneously by the Council and the European Parliament. That discussion is called a 'lecture'. As many as three readings can take place before the Council and Parliament agree on or reject a legislative proposal.

The Commission–Council–Parliament relationship is also known as the golden triangle. These three organs are the cornerstones of the decision-making process. Various advisory bodies, including the European Economic and Social Committee and the Committee of the Regions, circle around this.

Figure 1. The Golden Triangle

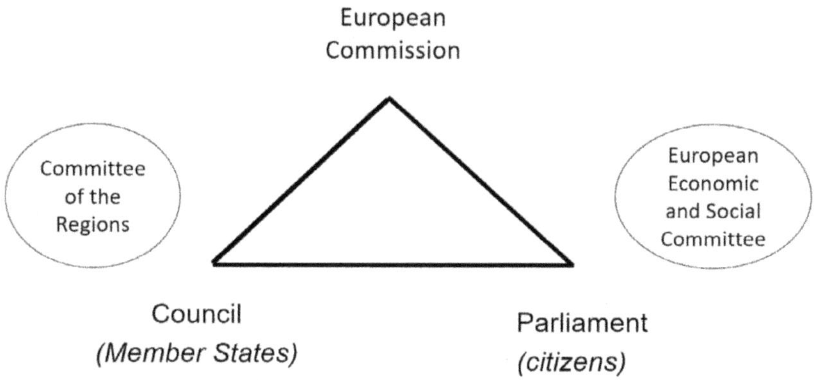

Source: Produced by the author.

Indeed, decisions must be made to safeguard the interests of all countries. Small countries often state that they do not have enough influence, while large countries feel that they contribute more and therefore should have more say. This led on the one hand to the concept of 'qualified majority', in which each country has similar weight based on population (population criterion), and on the other hand to the rule that a decision can only be taken if enough countries are behind it.

To properly understand that principle, we need to take a step back. After all, ab initio, every country had a right of veto, at least for strategic decisions. However, Europe could not function properly if everyone had the right to block a proposal that he or she did not like. It was enough for one country to leave the negotiating table to shut everything down. The European heads of government were also aware of this problem, and where previously most domains required unanimity, this principle was gradually eroded. The Unity Act was the starting point, with the introduction of the qualified majority principle. In the successive Treaties of Maastricht, Amsterdam and Nice, domains were transferred from unanimity to qualified majority.[13] The underlying motive was that the right of veto

13 In Nice, for example, 30 domains that previously had to be resolved by unanimity were transferred to qualified majority voting.

would render the European institutions unworkable if an expansion to 25–30 members were to take place.

For the most sensitive domains, unanimity remains the rule. Thus, external politics, EU membership, EU financial resources, taxes, social security, right of asylum, social cohesion, immigration, and even harmonization of national laws in the field of social security and social protection remain subject to the unanimity rule. By way of illustration, I refer to the European–Canada Trade Agreement (CETA Agreement), on which, due to the additional specificity of Belgium, the Walloon region exercised its veto. A region with 3.5 million inhabitants blocked a trade agreement between Canada and a region (Europe) with more than 500 million inhabitants. Absurdistan in full!

Or we might think of the disappointment of North Macedonia, which, as mentioned, changed its name to avoid Greece's veto, amended its constitution and held a referendum. The European Commission, the European Parliament and the European Council all suggested opening accession discussions, but were not prepared for France, which for quite unclear reasons – 'Europe is not ready' – vetoed it, much to Skopje's dismay. Tirana was also confronted with the French veto. A serious historic mistake by France, said then President of the European Commission Jean-Claude Juncker.[14] Could internal reasons have been at the root of the veto?

Finally, on procedural issues, or requests to the Commission to conduct studies or draw up proposals, the Council may decide by simple majority.

Qualified majority has now become the rule. But what does 'qualified' mean? Qualified majority, also known as double majority, is achieved when two conditions are met:

1. the proposal is supported by Member States representing at least 65% of the total EU population; and
2. 55% of Member States vote in favour (in practice that means 15 out of 27 Member States).

In addition, a blocking minority can exist if comprised at least four members of the Council representing more than 35% of the EU population.

In reaching its decision, the Council is assisted by more than 150 working groups and committees that help prepare the work of ministers

[14] European Council, October 2019. See 'EU's Juncker says blocking membership for North Macedonia and Albania "a historic error"', *Reuters*, 18.10.2019, https://www.reuters.com/article/us-eu-summit-balkans-juncker-error/eus-juncker-says-blocking-membership-for-north-macedonia-and-albania-a-historic-error-idUSKBN1WX1O5.

discussing the proposals in the various Council configurations. These working groups and committees are made up of officials from all Member States.

But in addition to the countries, citizens must also have a direct say. Jean Monnet said in his memoirs: 'Europe is not a cooperation between countries, but between citizens.'[15] The European Parliament has therefore rightly strived – particularly since direct elections began in 1979 – to be regarded as fully accountable. The main counter-argument was that the transfer of competence from the Member States to the European level was accompanied by a loss of democratic control.

Member States could decide at European level without Parliament having a real say. At the national level, however, all Member States are parliamentary democracies.[16] This means that every major decision has been analysed and discussed by Parliament, mostly through a bicameral legislature. The loss of democratic control in the transfer of power came to be known as the 'democratic deficit'.

This democratic deficit was slowly reduced by gradually strengthening Parliament's position. In this way, a more balanced decision-making system has developed. The position of Parliament was certainly strengthened with the Treaty of Amsterdam, as co-decision became the rule in legislation.[17] It is therefore primarily this procedure that I wish to highlight.

The European Parliament, like most national parliaments, uses the principle of absolute or simple majority. This simply means half plus one of the votes. But as Parliament has increasingly outgrown its infancy and evolved from a purely advisory body to a decision-making body, stricter requirements are placed on the presence of Members of the European Parliament (MEPs). This is why the treaty provides that in many cases the majority is not calculated on the basis of the effective members, but on the basis of the number of MEPs present. This explains why an empty parliament room in Strasbourg suddenly fills up at 12 noon: then the vote takes place. In addition, the treaty requires that in certain cases a two-thirds majority is necessary. For example, if Parliament wants to force the

---

15 'Nous ne coalisons pas des Etats, nous unissons des hommes', speech by Jean Monnet, Washington, 30 April 1952.

16 At least de jure; de facto they are often particracy.

17 For the sake of completeness, we mention that there are also three other procedures that have become de facto marginal. In the consultation procedure, the opinion of the Parliament is not binding. In the cooperation procedure, the European Parliament already has some more options to influence decision-making. In the assent procedure, on the other hand, a decision can only be reached if it has obtained Parliament's approval in advance.

Commission to resign, it requires a majority of two-thirds of the votes cast and also a majority of the MEPs.

It is interesting to note that the European Parliament functions by political party, or family. The two heavyweights in Parliament, the Christian Democratic and the Socialist parties, together represented the absolute majority until 2019.[18] After this time, to get half plus one, they then needed a third political party. It does not make life any easier, but my personal view is that in this way, additional views are taken into account, for example green or liberal approaches.

2.2. INTERPLAY BETWEEN THE EUROPEAN COUNCIL AND THE EUROPEAN PARLIAMENT

It is clear that once the proposal has left the Commission, the Council and the Parliament respectively, the representatives of the Member States and of the people hold sway. The co-decision procedure has become the rule. The procedure starts with the European Commission's proposal. After all, we stated earlier that the Commission has the right of initiative. This proposal is sent simultaneously to the Council and the Parliament and to the relevant advisory bodies (the Economic and Social Committee and the Committee of the Regions). As the name of the procedure suggests, the Council and the Parliament decide together and both have the same powers. The Council may in certain cases reach a political agreement pending Parliament's position at first reading; such an agreement is called a 'general orientation'. A Council general orientation could help speed up the legislative procedure and could even make it easier for both institutions to reach an agreement.

In this way, Parliament gets an idea of the Council's position before it itself adopts a position at first reading. However, the Council's final position can only be adopted after Parliament has adopted its own position at first reading. Parliament examines this proposal at first reading and forwards its opinion to the Council. If the Parliament does not propose amendments, or if the Council accepts the amendments proposed, the decision can already be finalized at first reading. De facto, 85% of decisions are taken at first reading. Second, and even third, readings are avoided as much as possible.

---

[18] For example, in the period 1999–2004, these two parties represented 66% of the seats; fifteen years later, in the period 2019–2024, that had shrunk to 44%.

When reference is made to a second reading, the Council adopts a common position on the basis of the Commission's proposal, the opinion of Parliament and the other institutions consulted, and, of course, on its own judgment, acting by a qualified majority. This common position goes to Parliament for a second reading. Parliament can then react in three ways:

1. Parliament approves the Council's position. The relevant decision is then adopted, in accordance with the common position. This approach is followed even if Parliament does not take a decision within three months.
2. Parliament rejects the position by an absolute majority. Then the legislative procedure is over and the decision is not taken.
3. Parliament makes further amendments to the common position. In that case, we are left with a third reading.

The Council can then adopt the common position as amended by Parliament. It must then accept all amendments. If, on the other hand, the Council rejects the amendments (or even just one amendment), the Council must convene the Conciliation Committee together with Parliament. The aim is to make a last-ditch effort to reach a compromise, based on the Council's common position and on the amendments requested by Parliament, that can find the required majority in both Council and Parliament. If the Conciliation Committee reaches such a compromise, the Council and Parliament must ratify the compromise at third reading within six weeks.

If the conciliation procedure fails, the decision is not adopted. We will then have the same consequences as the rejection of the common position. The procedure has come to an end and the Council no longer has the power to push through its position (as was the case before the Amsterdam Treaty).

2.3. LAWS, LAWS, LAWS

Despite the complicated and time-consuming procedures, the Commission has succeeded in developing a flood of law that has no equal. Laws are passed in all kinds of areas with the aim of improving the quality of life of Europeans. When we talk about 'laws' in Euro-jargon, we should distinguish between regulations, directives, decisions, recommendations and advice.

Regulations are legislative acts that apply automatically and in the same way in all EU countries from their entry into force. They are binding in their entirety in all EU countries.

Directives have a specific goal but give EU countries the freedom to decide for themselves how they want to achieve it. The EU countries must transpose directives into national legislation that must lead to the stated goal. Governments must notify these national transposition measures to the European Commission. The transposition into national law must be done within a certain period of time, usually within two years from the adoption of the directive. If an EU country fails to transpose a directive, the Commission can launch infringement proceedings against that country.

Decisions are binding legislative acts that apply to one or more EU countries, companies or individuals. The party/ies to which the decision applies must be notified and the decision will take effect at that time. Decisions do not need to be transposed into national law.

A recommendation allows the European institutions to express their views and propose a particular course of action, without creating legal obligations for those concerned. Recommendations are not binding.

Finally, opinions allow the EU institutions to make a statement, without this having any legal consequences for the advised body. This advice is not binding.

The legislation that is most felt in our daily lives is, of course, that which has to do with the internal market. If goods are allowed to move freely, naturally the consumer must have certain guarantees. Europe has therefore decided to label products that comply with European legislation. Many readers will already have noticed this certificate of conformity. Just look at the children's stuffed animal or the Barbie doll. They have, or at least should have, the CE marking: '*Conformité Européenne*'. This means that the toy complies with European technical standards and safety regulations.

Of course, this does not mean that some service in Europe has tested the stuffed animal or the Barbie doll. It means that the producer declares that the product has been produced in accordance with European legislation. By means of sampling, this statement is tested against goods on the shelves, and the non-compliant ones are removed. Consumers thus have the quasi-certainty that CE-labelled goods meet technical standards and safety regulations, and that the producer can sell the goods freely within the European market, and so reach more than 500 million consumers. The former 'national' regulations have therefore been replaced by European regulations, making life easier for both consumers and producers. The consumer also has the guarantee that such products must be repaired or replaced free of charge if they break within two years of purchase. This 'easier life' has been removed in the UK due to Brexit. The UKCA (UK Conformity Assessed) marking is a new UK product marking that is used for goods placed on the market in Great Britain (England, Wales and Scotland). It covers most goods which previously required the CE marking, known as 'new approach' goods. The UKCA marking came into effect on 1 January 2021. However, to allow businesses time to adjust to the new requirements, a transitory period still enabling the use of the CE marking was foreseen until 1 January 2023.

In addition to the CE label, there is also recognition of products based on their geographical origin, such as English whisky, Welsh leeks, Scotch beef, calvados, cider from Normandy or Brittany, Gouda from Holland, or *jambon d'Ardenne*. We call this a protected geographical indication (PGI). A variant is recognition based on the protected destination of origin (PDO) when a product is fully processed in a traditional way within a certain area, such as Shetland lamb, Single Gloucester, North Holland Gouda, Kanterkaas, Greek feta or Italian Parma ham, or even Walloon péket, Flemish country wine, Brocciu Corse, *vin d'Anjou*, Brie de Meaux, Herve cheese or the Flemish Brabant grape. In addition, there is also the simple geographical indication (GI) such as Irish whiskey, rum from Martinique or Guadeloupe, or Hasselt genever. Finally, there are traditional guaranteed specialities (TGS) such as traditional Bramley apple pie filling, mozzarella, Dutch buddies, *jamón serrano*, Old Gueuze Lambic, moules de Bouchot, or Berthoud's cheese recipe.

Europhobes will of course find enough material in this approach to ridicule Europe's bureaucracy. And sometimes they have a point. For example, in its legislative zeal, Europe regulated the standards for 26 types of fruit and vegetables.[19] For example, the curvature of cucumbers was laid down in a regulation and led to the division of cucumbers into four classes. For the 'extra' class, the maximum height of the curvature may be 10 mm per 10 cm of the length of the cucumber. Slightly curved cucumbers, with a maximum height of the curvature of 20 mm per 10 cm of the length of the cucumber, belong to a lower class.[20]

Fruits and vegetables that did not conform to the Eurocrat's yardstick or compass had to be destroyed. Bureaucracy at its best. However, Europe itself realized that not everything needs to be harmonized and reversed its steps. Since 2009, it has been allowed to sell all fruits and vegetables,

---

19 In particular, apricots, artichokes, asparagus, aubergines, avocados, beans, Brussels sprouts, carrots, cauliflowers, celery, cherries, chicory, courgettes, cucumbers, garlic, unshelled hazelnuts, head cabbage, leeks, melons, mushrooms, onions, peas, plums, spinach, walnuts in the shell and watermelons.

20 Commission Regulation (EEC) No 1677/88 of 15 June 1988 laying down quality standards for cucumbers.

regardless of their size or shape. The standards for 26 types of fruits and vegetables have been revoked. Since then, we can again find abnormal or naturally curvy, branched, knobbly, bumpy and crooked fruits and vegetables on the shelves of the greengrocer or organic farmer. This revision meant the abolition of unnecessary bureaucracy, more freedom of choice for the consumer and less waste: the products with different shapes no longer need to be thrown away.

It is worth noting that many Member States had requested these regulations and subsequently opposed their abolition. The legislation provided for a classification of fruits and vegetables for storage, transport and shelf life, but the Commission was of course the villain in the story. And thus, the myth of an otherworldly, all-regulatory bureaucracy was born, a myth that has survived for a long time and is still often quoted in speeches by Europhobes as a jab at Europe's over-regulation.

Specific marketing standards continue to apply for eleven products, which make up 75% of the value of EU trade: apples, citrus fruits, kiwis, lettuce, nectarines, peaches, pears, peppers, strawberries, table grapes and tomatoes. However, Member States may also allow derogations from the standards or even exempt them from the marketing standards for these products if an appropriate label has been affixed to them when they are sold in shops. In practice, this means that an apple that does not meet the standard may still be sold in stores, provided that the label 'product intended for processing' or a similar statement is included. But perception has a long life.

Box 1. On condoms and breasts

The urge to standardize the curvature of the cucumber was the basis for many myths about Brussels bureaucracy. The British newspaper *The Sun* ran an article about Eurocrats who were working on a regulation to regulate the length of condoms, while not paying sufficient attention to cultural differences. The newspaper stated that, on the basis of subsidiarity, Member States should be able to take into account the different characteristics of the male member.[21] Various newspapers subsequently took up the message and a new myth was born. The reality was very different: the European Committee for Standardization was working on the safety requirements (not the length requirements) that a condom must meet.

[21] 'EU to push for standard condom size', *The Sun*, 19 October 1994.

To take another example, Europe was working on an EU directive that employers should be responsible for ensuring that all staff who work outside of the home are not over-exposed to the sun. This was in an effort to reduce skin cancer. The directive suggested that this could include providing workers with sunscreen or allowing them to wear protective clothing. The British media interpreted this initiative as saying that Brussels bureaucrats were about to put bureaucratic guidelines on the exposed busts of British busty barmaids because wearing too much cleavage was considered a health hazard. 'Hands off our barmaids' boobs,' the newspaper headline ran, with accompanying photos of busty barmaids.[22] There was no mention of barmaids at all in the proposed directive, busty or not. The smear campaign meant that the proposal never saw the light of day.

2.4. POINTING FINGERS

In addition to the drive to harmonize, Europe, like many of its Member States, is developing a society where 'it is forbidden to'. The urge to prohibit, which is usually introduced with the best intentions, leads to a stifling of society where nothing is allowed. Moreover, the data economy, a phenomenon that developed more quickly during the COVID-19 crisis, ensures that everything is mapped and visualized. Data can say with no equivocation whose smartphone my smartphone spent the night with. Once everything has been mapped out, the use to which it is put determines the ethical dimension of the event.

Let us take a few examples. Have you seen what is on a pack of cigarettes? Patients dying of lung cancer. And yet smoking continues almost unabated.[23] Most readers will probably approve of this regulation, but it opens the door to the regulation society. Insurance companies may vary life insurance or hospitalization insurance premiums based on the smoking habits of the insured. A few decades ago, we were much freer and could decide for ourselves what we allowed ourselves, what we did not. Do not be too lazy or frightened to think for yourself was the message of Kantian enlightenment. Now they are thinking in our place.

---

22 'Leave our boobs alone', *Irish Examiner*, 17 May 2017.

23 In 2020 there were 1.3 billion smokers worldwide; five years earlier, in 2015, it was 1.32 billion, so a very slight decrease (source: World Health Organization, 2021, https://www.who.int/news/item/16-11-2021-tobacco-use-falling-who-urges-countries-to-invest-in-helping-more-people-to-quit-tobacco).

Breastfeeding is good, health gurus say. There too, we should leave the choice to mothers. Inform, sensitize, but do not take mothers for beings without any judgement. In an analogy to packs of cigarettes, it is forbidden to place a photo of a smiling baby on a box of milk powder. After all, the European Union has banned producers from promoting powdered milk with 'images that can idealize the use of those products'. Europe wants to prevent mothers from being encouraged in this way to stop breastfeeding.

Herve cheese or the Parmigiano Reggiano may be protected brands, but that does not prevent their production methods or ingredients from being criticized. Unpasteurized milk in particular has been a target. Raw milk is said to pose health risks. In an effort to establish safety rules that apply across Europe, traditional cooking methods are banned or restricted. The local population usually looks with great incomprehension at the Brussels Eurocrats who suddenly state that methods that have been used for generations are now no longer allowed for health reasons.

Parmigiano Reggiano is made according to traditional methods from fresh, raw milk. After the cheese has set, brine is added. The cheese is left to ripen for 25 days. Few bacteria survive this brine bombardment. And since the cheese has been made in exactly the same way for centuries, it has also been known for just as long that it is not only tasty, but also safe. Of course, everything can be pasteurized and sterilized, but what is left of taste? Or as Slow Food sums it up in their manifesto in support of raw milk cheese: 'It is true that pasteurization kills bacteria and pleases large companies, but it also kills the taste and smell of the region that characterizes every cheese.'[24] I could not agree more!

Incidentally and worth mentioning, whereas vegans renounce cheese, it is still on the menu for vegetarians, a discipline to which, by the way, I also adhere. However, most Parmesan cheeses, like many others, contain animal rennet. After all, to make cheese from milk, the milk has to be made very thick using rennet, which usually comes from the stomach lining of a dead calf. Cheese is therefore anything but vegetarian.

After health considerations, environmental considerations are the second major area of daily life to regulate. In 2018, Europe decided to ban regular screw caps on bottles and only allow click caps on plastic bottles.

---

24 www.slowfood.com.

From now on, plastic bottles must be made in such a way that the top cannot be detached. The European Commission got rid of the screw cap as too often they ended up in the environment. These sports and snap caps have already led to various complaints from consumers because children in particular have a hard time opening them.

All disposable plastic will also be banned: plastic straws, cutlery, plates, stirrers and balloon sticks will be banned, and other single-use plastic products will be restricted. The measures affect the ten types of plastic waste most commonly found on European beaches. Fishermen are also asked to hand in their old fishing nets, which often otherwise end up at the bottom of the sea. And this is right, because about 45% of the plastic waste in the North Sea appears to come from fishermen.

In any case, these are golden times for lobbyists and climate activists. But overshooting is counter-productive. I think the environment benefits more from a balance between the environment and economy than from a conflict between them. This may be akin to the proverbial swearing in church, especially considering the planet is screaming for attention through floods and fires, but even in this context, we all benefit from balanced thinking rather than acting on emotional predictions of catastrophe. Catastrophe gurus do not always do the planet a service, and are just as likely to provide food for climate sceptics.

Exactly 50 years ago, the report of the Club of Rome, of which I was a strong supporter, predicted that within 50 years – in 2022 – all raw materials would be exhausted.[25] As it turns out, the hypothesis of exponential population growth coupled with linear technological progress did not materialize. Economic growth was much faster than the report had foreseen, and the exhaustion has not (yet) occurred. So, let us be careful not to undermine the credibility of the forecasts, with unrealistic underlying hypotheses and hyper-extrapolating models.

Finally, we must avoid shifting the blame from one generation to another. Generation X had to create wealth to survive. Generation Z questioning from the perspective of prosperity and pointing out the overload on the planet is a very good thing, but the finger of blame is not helpful.

---

25 D.H. Meadows, D.L. Meadows, J. Randers and W.W. Behrens III, *Limits to Growth, Report of the Club of Rome*, MIT, 1972.

3. THE EUROCRACY: FROM START-UP TO JUGGERNAUT

A bureaucracy is an impersonal machine in which the individual freedom of civil servants is lost.

Max Weber[26]

The functioning of European administration is organized and implemented by a combination of civil servants, often scornfully called Eurocrats, politically elected persons (in the directly elected European Parliament) and politically appointed persons (the Commissioners and the members of the Committees). The entire apparatus that was originally lean and mean has grown into a gigantic bureaucracy. The inherent inflation of bureaucracy, of which Max Weber warned, has taken concrete shape here.

3.1. HOW IT STARTED

I was not involved at the beginning of the European story. I myself started in the Commission 30 years after the Treaty of Rome. It had always been my dream to work for Europe and that is precisely why I read for a Master's degree at the College of Europe in Bruges and took part in the so-called 'competitive concours'. I remember that we were 55,000 candidates for 35 'vacancies'. And when I got the verdict that I was there and could start, the existential doubt set in. In the meantime, I had become a credit manager at a large bank, earned a good living, enjoyed my job and for me 'the sky was the limit,' said the then CEO of the bank. And last but not least, I lived by the sea, in West Flanders and would have to exchange my high-quality lifestyle for a job in Brussels and choose between living in Brussels and commuting, braving the daily traffic jams or taking the constantly delayed and overcrowded train. After much hesitation, I negotiated a status of leave without pay at the bank and started to work in Brussels, commuting from Oostduinkerke, a coastal village 130 miles from Brussels. Now people

26 M. Weber, 'Os Fundamentos da Organização Burocrática: uma Construção do Tipo Ideal' ['The Foundations of the Bureaucratic Organization: A Construction of the Ideal Type'], AAVV, *Sociologia da Burocracia [Sociology of Bureaucracy]*, Zahar Editores (Fundamentals of bureaucratic organisation), 1966.

would say that my ecological footprint was socially irresponsible, but back then, nobody had heard of that concept.

Once there in Brussels, I realized that my existential doubt was actually quite ridiculous. Almost all my colleagues had moved from their native country with all their belongings. The international atmosphere was – and I still think is – sublime. And the first time I got my payslip, I thought it was a mistake. My wages were more than double what I earned as a credit manager.

Considering my background in philosophy – yes, I studied Thomistic philosophy for four years in Leuven; nobody is perfect – I wondered why the risks were so high. I had the chance to speak with colleagues who were there from the start and had by then almost reached the age of retirement. They opened my eyes. It was a start-up, they said, in 1958. Most were not willing to take that risk, because nobody thought the project would last. Besides, analogue projects in the world had all been short-lived. So, nobody wanted to give up their job to work for the European Commission. A Frenchman told me that he telephoned former fellow students to ask them to come and work for the Commission. And yes, they were allowed to start the next day. They then had to move and come to work in Brussels – of all places. But that was temporary, it was said at the time, because if the project really took off, the final place of work would be Nice. Yes, the Côte d'Azur is a much more attractive place, if only because of the climate.

When it later became clear that the Commission would never go to Nice, but would stay in Brussels for the time being – and 'for the time being' became indefinite – this was a great disappointment, especially for the Italians and the French. They even required a solar premium in compensation. However, this requirement was never accepted. After 50 years, Brussels was chosen as the definitive location. They had left their sunny homes and their family for a risky job in a fragile start-up in the grey, unsafe, badly governed city of Brussels. Add to that the fact that the work was in an international institution and had to be done in an international and multilingual context, and the legitimacy for the high wages was clear. At the time, no one could foresee that the originally small start-up with six members and minimal powers would grow into a gigantic juggernaut.

3.2. THE REALM OF MYTHS

For years now, especially via social media, reports have appeared regularly that Eurocrats are retiring at the age of 50, with a monthly pension of €9,000. It is called outrageous, and rightly so. Only, it does not match reality.

It is what is today called fake news. In addition, other myths, such as Eurocrats who make purchases without paying VAT or are exempted from taxes, do not correspond to reality. It is therefore important to take a look at facts and figures. So, time for a fact check.

Eurocrats do indeed have a generous pension, especially if you compare it with, for example, the United Kingdom, Belgium or France, where the pensions are quite low. The relatively high pensions for Eurocrats are the result of several factors:

- For every year worked, the Eurocrat is entitled to a 1.8% pension with a maximum of 70% of the salary. De facto, a full career is 39 years.
- The pension is calculated on the last year worked (compared to, for example, the last ten years for civil servants and the entire career for employees in Belgium, or the 25 'best' years in France).
- The Eurocrat retires at 66 (compared to 67 in Belgium and the Netherlands, 66 (67 in 2026) in the UK and 62 in France). The system is flexible, with a kind of bonus–malus system. After all, the Eurocrat can already retire from the age of 58 ('pensionable' age). In the case of 'early retirement', the pension is reduced by 3.5% for each year that the Eurocrat retires early. But the Eurocrat can also continue to work until the age of 67 or even 70. Those who do this will receive a bonus of 1.5% per 'extra' year worked. Such a pension bonus was also introduced in Belgium, but has since been abolished. It still exists, for example, in France, where it pays to work after retirement age, especially for those who have worked for less than 42 years.

Suppose a university-educated Eurocrat retires at age 66 and started working for the European institutions at age 30 (most people start later). He/she then has 36 working years, which entitles him/her to 64.8% of the final wage as a pension. To calculate the pension, we take the final wage and multiply it by this coefficient. Generous, yes. But in line with the myths, no. In addition, for this pension he/she contributes to a pension fund. Each month, 11.6% is deducted from the Eurocrat's salary. The employer adds two-thirds to this, resulting in 34.8%.

With regard to taxes, as with all international institutions, there is a system whereby taxes are paid to the employer. The Eurocrat therefore pays taxes to the European institutions. Again, compared to many Europeans, the Eurocrat pays few taxes. The question, of course, is whether the Eurocrat pays too little, or most Europeans pay too much. Personally, I go for the latter option. The tax rates are based on a progressive rate increasing to 45%.

And VAT is paid like everyone else, with one exception. The Eurocrat who comes from another country and starts working as a Eurocrat can make purchases in the year of installation that are exempt from VAT. This sometimes leads to absurd situations where the installation year is optimized with frequent purchases whereby many Eurocrats accumulate debt burdens. Wage garnishment is therefore a common occurrence in the Commission. The Eurocrat therefore does not pay national taxes on the salary paid by the European institutions, but does pay all other taxes, such as withholding and real estate tax, car taxes, and so on.

Anyone who comes from another country is also entitled to an allowance of 16% of the salary as compensation for leaving his/her home country, as an expatriate.

3.3. DIFFERENT CATEGORIES

As in any public institution, there are civil servants appointed for life, temporary civil servants (three to six years) and contract workers, who are offered a temporary contract, but with different conditions. This translates into various contracts. Broadly speaking, there are three types:

- grade A – civil servants: these are the highest categories, where at least a university degree is expected; they start at A5 status and can progress to A16 (commissioner and directors-general);
- grade AD – officials: these are posts that do not require a university degree; and
- contract workers: depending on diploma and experience, ranging from group 1 to group 4.

The same rules apply in all European institutions. All the institutions together employ a total of 55,000 staff, of whom 58% are based in Brussels. The rest are spread over many countries such as Luxembourg, France (Strasbourg) and in fact all over the world (in the European representative offices). Most (45,000) are civil servants and the rest (10,000) are contract workers, mostly working in the European agencies. Three-fifths, i.e. 32,000, work at the Commission, 700 at the European Economic and Social Committee, 600 at the Committee of the Regions, 3,500 at the Council of the European Union, and finally 7,500 at the European Parliament. These are the numbers of officials. These are not to be confused with Members of the European Parliament or members of the advisory bodies. There are also 4,300 translators and 800 interpreters associated with the European institutions.

Indeed, there are also elected representatives of the people (Members of the European Parliament) or members designated by society (Members of the Economic and Social Committee) and members designated by their region (Members of the Committee of the Regions). Often the press lumps all these categories together, which sometimes leads to confusion. However, Europe is very transparent in this regard. Let us take a look at the statutes.

3.4. HOW MUCH DOES A EUROCRAT EARN?

The Commission, like most international institutions, is very transparent about remuneration. A starting policy officer (with a university degree) at the Commission earns about €5,000 gross per month. This amount can rise to a maximum of more than €21,000 gross per month, but only 40 of the 33,000 civil servants earn that.[27] Eurocrats are paid 'only' twelve months a year, in other words, they are not entitled to holiday pay and do not receive an end-of-year bonus. By the way, since the Eurocrat pays personal income tax to his employer and not to the national state, he or she is also not eligible for national tax deductions, such as tax benefits when taking out a mortgage loan.

Adam Smith in his *Wealth of Nations* states that the principle of the invisible hand means that we all earn the same amount if we add the pecuniary elements together with the non-pecuniary elements. He gives the example of the executioner who naturally has to take a high wage to compensate for his status. Can we say by analogy – and as it is often argued – that the European institutions are golden cages full of overpaid, frustrated officials, who stay there for the love of money? Yes, this exists. In order to avoid this as much as possible, mobility is encouraged, which of course offers many possibilities in such a large institution.

Moreover, one can also take up to twelve years' leave without pay. As the description implies, one is not paid, and not promoted, but one can go back to the Commission at any time if and/or when required. For example, one can start a business and return if that fails. Or one can – as in my case – perform another function. I myself was on leave for ten years without pay,

---

27 The most recent figures can be found at https://euemployment.eu/how-much-do-eu-officials-earn/.

successively as head of staff in Wallonia, federal head of staff in Belgium and in Flanders, secretary-general in Flanders and finally director-general of One Laptop per Child (OLPC), a spin-off of the famous Massachusetts Institute of Technology (MIT). Where else can one afford that luxury?

By the way, in my Flemish positions I was most troubled by narrow-mindedness. I am a proud Fleming in the world. Those who do not travel think they are always right, I thought, referring to Pablo Neruda, when, as was the case in most meetings, the Flemish perspective was the only angle and dogmatism often stood in the way of efficiency. The fact that people wished me good morning in different languages, both at MIT and in the European institutions, was a nice start to the day for me. In Flanders, only one language was heard in the morning, if one said good morning at all. Take the elevator in Flanders and take it in Europe or in Wallonia (the southern region of Belgium where plenty of kisses on the cheek were given in greeting, at least before the COVID-19 crisis) and the cultural differences are immediately apparent. I call it a cultural elevator pitch. In the MIT elevator, everyone said, 'Hey Rudy, how are you today?' I kept wondering how they knew my name. I prefer the slightly more in-depth European contacts, but still with a smile. The acidification of society that can often be read on the faces of civil servants does not, to me, seem to promote productivity – or as the Chinese proverb says: 'If you can't smile, don't open a shop.'

But back to the Commission, literally. As a financing specialist, the Commission contacted me and asked if I was still considering coming back, as they urgently needed someone to take over the financing of space policy. For the record, I was then deploying my One Laptop per Child computers in Timbuktu, Mali, and came back to Brussels. I knew nothing about space and satellites, but financing, that is my thing. I immediately accepted because I rarely, if ever, say no to new challenges. After ten years of absence, I re-joined the ranks of the European Commission. Where else is that possible?

It was a disorienting existential experience. I saw a lot of people I had not seen for ten years and I thought to myself: they have all grown older. So had I, of course. And although I had sworn never to become chief of staff again – my last position in that capacity in Flanders was my least enjoyable professional experience – I accepted the position of chief of private office to the President of the Economic and Social Committee, a mandated position from the European employers. When my tenure ended, I considered working full time as a professor, but human resources asked me what might motivate me to stay. I said scornfully: 'No responsibility for staff, total freedom and only strategic files', knowing that this was a quite impossible requirement. The next day I got an email, with a laughing smiley, suggesting a role as a member of the chief economist team with responsibilities for space, financing and taxation. I now travel around the world, give conferences on various topics in various languages, have a great time and get paid well. Again, who says that working for the Commission is a golden cage that one does not leave simply for pecuniary reasons? And then came COVID-19 who temporarily converted me into a 'zoomby'. The time saved by virtual conferences was not compensated for by the job satisfaction associated with human contact and pleasant business trips. Fortunately these restarted post-COVID, albeit often in hybrid forms.

3.5. THE CRIPPLING BUREAUCRACY?

People with a private spirit often fear the switch to the public sector. A bureaucracy has hardly any key performance indicators (KPIs), as known in the private sector, and at the end of the day it is not always easy to estimate exactly what has been achieved or not. This is indeed a tricky point. And yes, the bureaucracy can be heavy and paralysing, but with enough 'guts and creativity'[28] one can still achieve things, certainly at a European level, where the administration is not duplicated – literally – by gigantic political cabinets.

By way of illustration, I would like to list three achievements that I can put on my European record in the Commission. Firstly, I designed and implemented the Joint European Ventures (JEV) programme with the aim of stimulating European companies to set up joint ventures with companies from other European countries. The Commission funded the feasibility study and if an investment was made on that basis, it was also supported. It is a means to allow companies to enjoy the internal market beyond purely commercial relationships.

I also put the concept of business angels on the European map. I had heard about it at a conference in the UK, where the idea had already implemented quite successfully. I co-founded the European Business Angel Network (EBAN), with the Commission budget. It was the first Business Angel Network (BAN) active in Europe. Twenty years later, 400 BANs are now active in Europe and the 30,000 active investors fund 3,600 start-ups every year. Wikipedia calls me the 'father of European business angels'.

---

28 This is how I defined entrepreneurship in my book *Entrepreneurship: no guts, no glory*, Intersentia, 2020.

Recently I conceived a programme for financing scale-ups. 45% of successful start-ups leave Europe in their scale-up phase because they cannot find the large amount of money they need to grow further (on average €15–25 million) in Europe. With the new programme, ESCALAR (European Scale-up Action for Risk Capital), we can double the capacity of the venture capital funds, partly by attracting private investors, such as pension funds. Additionally, the programme provides for a risk limitation linked to a limitation of the possible return. Again, I did not invent it, I copied it, this time from the United States.

Job satisfaction, earning good money, being creative, changing the world, being able to leave at any time ... and return, and moreover combine that with teaching (I have been teaching at Ghent University and the University of Nancy for over twenty years) – no, it is not a golden cage for me. But everyone has to decide this for him/herself, of course, as long as it remains a choice for the right reasons. My case is probably not the most representative, as confirmed by a Eurocrat who I met at the quarterly reception where top Eurocrats meet the corporate world – and I quote: 'I'm Belgian, over 50 and male, so I combine all disabilities, how do you want me to be happy in the Commission without any prospects.' Waiting for his retirement and counting his days like Robinson Crusoe is what he believes is his fate. It reminded me of one of my directors – a 40-year-old PhD in Economics – when I was secretary-general in Flanders, who said to me: 'Secretary-General, don't count on me anymore, I've had it here, but unfortunately, I can't leave because of my retirement privileges.' Then he took a crumpled piece of paper from his pocket with his pension calculation: 'If you can tell me where I can have that, I'm gone. As long as you can't do that, don't ask me or I'll fall sick.' When I gave him a task, he carried out his threat.

By the way, as secretary-general, with responsibility for an administration of 1,100 officials, I netted one-third of what I earn at the Commission. I did have a car with a driver, meal vouchers, a thirteenth and fourteenth month and, theoretically at least, bonuses. In fact, I have never had the last one as I wanted to reform the administration and did not obey ministerial orders that I considered an abuse of public funds. But moreover, my job satisfaction in the Commission was three times greater and I was not bullied by jealous ministers. But that is another, old and regrettable story that illustrates once again the narrow-mindedness of Flanders. We really are victims of a cutthroat society mentality.[29]

---

29 For those who are interested, I refer to my book *Wedervaren van een Cabinettard [Experience of a Cabinettard]*, Roularta Business Books, 2008.

3.6. HOW MUCH DOES A MEMBER OF THE EUROPEAN PARLIAMENT EARN?

It should be a positive choice to become a Member of the European Parliament, MEP in the jargon. But far too often the Parliament is an old people's home for side-lined politicians. Many MEPs are 'end of careers'. The average age of an MEP is over 50. Many of them become an MEP because political 'friends' want to get rid of them at regional or national level. As a kind of reward or compensation, they then become a Member of the European Parliament. Too bad for the image of Europe and in particular for the European Parliament.

Even worse is that many MEPs are against 'Europe'. Members of the European Parliament come from 190 national parties and group themselves at European level into seven political 'families'. Three of those families are not really European-minded and represent 134 of the 705 members, or almost one in five. It is like a company where one in five of the members of the general meeting is against the company. Just think of the Le Pen family: father, daughter, niece … they were all in the European Parliament even though they are against Europe. In the Parliament restaurant it is a bizarre sight to see all the Le Pens systematically and daily at one table. Nigel Farage, the man who can be proud to have made the Brexit vote a reality and who has in this way caused enormous damage to Europe, also remained in the European Parliament after the referendum.

Whether or not you are elected depends mainly on where you are on the list. Promising a politician first place is often motivation to leave national politics, since one is sure of a seat. Elections hardly matter. Michel Rocard, at odds with Mitterrand, left national politics and remained in the European Parliament until the blessed age of 77; (former) presidential candidates Jean-Marie Le Pen, his daughter Marie Le Pen and Jean-Luc Mélenchon also took seats in Parliament.

The former Flemish Minister-President of the Kingdom of Belgium – yes, Belgium has one King and six presidents – Kris Peeters was 'asked' by the party chairman, after his catastrophic elections in Antwerp, to pull the European list, as it is called. Another example of the primacy of particracy over democracy. He would only last eighteen months before claiming the open position of Vice-President of the European Investment Bank, as the Dutch, who could occupy the post if Belgium left it empty, threatened to appoint someone themselves if the Belgians did not agree on a candidate. Or consider Geert Bourgeois, another former Flemish Minister-President, who was offered an 'appointment' at the European Parliament in order to make room at the

Flemish level for the next Flemish Minister-President from the same right-wing party. Unfortunately, all political parties are sick in the same bed, even those who carry so-called good governance high on their party banner.

Contrary to national parliaments, anyone who leaves the European Parliament and gives up his seat to a *suppléant* cannot retake his seat even if he or she chooses to. I think the fact that one cannot return is a positive ruling as it avoids 'revolving doors'. But additionally, it shows respect for the successor, and also not simply serving to keep the proverbial seat warm. Ultimately, it should not just be about the posts, although unfortunately this is often the case. Politics should be a passion, not a well-paid job, and preferably lifelong.

What also fuels anti-politics is that people go on the list, but make it plain to the public – clearly or not – that they are not a real candidate in the least and therefore never intend to sit in the European Parliament. This shows a total lack of respect for the voter.

It is therefore not surprising that citizens are indifferent to political events, and indifference, according to Hannah Arendt, heralds the end of democracy. The figures in Table 1 below at European level, illustrated by the Netherlands and France, two almost neighbouring countries, are worrying in this regard and make the trend abundantly clear. And the UK figures clearly show the apathy of the British citizens for the European Union. Many Europeans have become Europe-apathetic. Moreover, the European averages are slightly distorted by countries such as Belgium, where voting is compulsory. By the way, 'only' 88% of Belgians voted, which means that as many as 12% would risk a fine rather than fulfil their voting obligation.

Table 1. Turnout (in %) for the European parliamentary elections

Year	EU	Netherlands	France	UK
1979	62	58	61	32
1984	59	51	57	33
1989	58	47	49	36
1994	57	36	53	36
1999	49	30	47	24
2004	45	39	43	38
2009	43	37	41	35
2014	42	37	43	36
2019	50	41	50	37

Source: Compiled by the author.

Insiders attribute the positive turnaround in 2019, after decades of declining interest, to the Brexit fuss. Unfortunately, the larger proportion of nationalists probably correlates to the larger turnout. Could the fact that many politicians accept a mandate as a career path and remain, even if they are against Europe, have something to do with the rules? Before giving the figures, it is important to state that membership of the European Parliament cannot really be considered a full-time job. The amount of time one spends on parliamentary work is highly variable. The net salary is the same for all members, €7,300 net per month.[30] That is a fixed wage. In addition, MEPs receive an extra €338 per day if they attend meetings. That is why there are always attendance lists at the entrance of the meeting rooms where parliamentarians are queuing. This should cover the costs associated with being present. A Member of Parliament who is present two or three days a week can quickly see his/her salary increase by €2,500 per month.

In addition, there is a general expenditure allowance (GEA) of €4,342 per month. This theoretically covers the costs of purchase and maintenance of computer equipment, administration, telephone and shipping. The amount is halved for members who attend less than half the number of plenary sittings in a parliamentary year. Expenses do not have to be proven and any money that is not spent is not required to be refunded. Naturally, costs related to commuting to and from work are also reimbursed. For those who travel by car, the reimbursement is €0.50 per kilometre, supplemented with a travel expense allowance. In short, a nice little earner for most MEPs. This comes on top of the generous pension system, whereby every effective year as an MEP leads to 3.5% of the salary as a pension. Twenty years of European Parliamentary work leads to the maximum of 70% of the final salary as a pension. in most cases, this pension comes on top of other, national, pension schemes.

But back to the GEA. Transparency requirements spurred the European Parliament to put in place robust financial control mechanisms, carry out an internal audit of the general expenditure allowance, make the GEA spending information fully transparent and also publish these details in open-source format. However, the proposal to prove cost-effectiveness was not accepted by MEPs. They realized that the 'lump sum' is by no means justified. Frederique Ries, a former news presenter who was able to cash in on her fame with a parliamentary mandate, when questioned by the media about what she did with the expense allowance, came up with nothing

---

[30] Data for 2022. For current data, see https://www.europarl.europa.eu/news/en/faq/12/salaries-and-pensions.

better than buying binders with it. I invite the reader to calculate how many binders she would have had to buy each month to justify the expense allowance. But she is not an isolated case. All parliamentarians know that they cannot justify these costs. It should therefore come as no surprise that they comprehensively rejected the proposal to make payment based on actual expenses. This is yet another example of how personal interest takes precedence over the public interest, and is a source of citizen apathy towards 'pocket-lining' politics.[31]

Abuse of budgets intended to finance assistants is also commonplace. The Front National was ordered to repay European funds that were misused for personal assistants. But Francois Bayrou's MoDem and Jean-Luc Mélenchon's France insoumise were also likewise discredited. It did not do the tarnished reputation of the French in Europe much good, after Edith Cresson's analogous scandal that led to the fall of the Santer Commission.

In addition to its elected members, the European Parliament also has many officials. Those consist on the one hand of the assistants to the MEPs, and on the other hand of officials who are responsible for the organization of the Parliament. The relationship between the MEPs and the latter is not always clear. The European Parliament has become a bureaucracy in its own right, led with an invisible hand by the secretary-general in the mould of Sir Humphrey on the British television series *Yes, Minister*, as one MEP lamented.[32]

3.7. HOW MUCH DOES A MEMBER OF THE ADVISORY COMMITTEES EARN?

This statute for parliamentarians not only causes annoyance to citizens, but colleagues from the advisory bodies are also suspicious of it. After all, the members of the Economic and Social Committee or the members of the Committee of the Regions only receive an allowance for commuting expenses and an allowance per meeting, the rules being the same as for Members of the European Parliament. So, they receive no wages. They are supposed to be paid by their organization, for example by their trade union or business association.

---

31 98.4% of all MEPs in 2014, including departing ones from the last mandate, used the full amount of their general expenditure allowance, see http://transparency.eu/wp-content/uploads/2017/05/GEA_Briefing_final.pdf.

32 D.J. Eppink, *Het Rijk der Kleine Koningen [The Kingdom of the Little Kings]*, Pelckmans, 2015.

The European Economic and Social Committee was founded in 1957 with the aim of giving civil society a voice in European decision-making. The Committee therefore issues opinions on the Commission's proposals. The Committee is not really a model of dynamism. More than a third of the members have already retired and top up their 'expense allowances' with a pension. The Economic and Social Committee has 329 members, neatly distributed between employers (group I), employees (group II) and third parties (group III: diversity, i.e. women's lobbies, trade associations, organizations for the disabled, etc.). Once a month they all come to Brussels for a week to vote in plenary opinions on the various Commission proposals. A new chairman is appointed every two and a half years on a rotation basis across the three groups. The many missions also always consist of a delegation of a multiple of three, whereby each group has the right to delegate someone. Notably, for the many exotic trips, the group chairmen are lobbied very hard to enable the privileged to travel. After all, the Committee also discusses international relations, so missions to China, South America or the Antilles are commonplace. A former French Committee chairman, Henri Malosse, vehemently criticized luxury travel, which he ironically described as visiting fictional partners around the world.[33] That could be seen as quite the accusation from someone who was for decades himself a member before he came to hold the highest position.

Since many members are well into their retirement, and as this often goes hand in hand with health problems, a nurse is always present in the room during plenary sessions to assist the most acute cases. Europe at its best.

The Committee of the Regions is more recent, i.e. from 1994. Its creation had a twofold purpose. Firstly, about three-quarters of EU legislation is implemented at a decentralized level, which made it useful to involve representatives of local and regional authorities in the development of new European rules. Secondly, there was a fear that the public would become increasingly distant from the process of European integration. One way to reduce that distance was to give the elected governing bodies closest to the citizens a role in policy-making. This is because the regions, especially those fighting for more autonomy, were frustrated that Europe only negotiated at the level of the Member States. This is why a new advisory committee was created to represent the voice of the regions. With a budget of €100 million, it is the smaller and younger brother of the Economic

33 H. Malosse, in B. Lacoux, *CESE: ces conseillers européens trop bien payés pour voyager*, in Tous contribuable, Newsletter, 21 July 2021.

and Social Committee. Its members are often better known, as they represent municipalities, cities and regions. Like the Economic and Social Committee, it has 329 members.

Both committees are housed in the same building, although the tension between the two is only just about manageable. The European Economic and Social Committee has still not been able to accept the creation of a new advisory body. Since both committees seek visibility, it is, for example, impossible to have a common reception desk in the building. Woe to the visitor who makes a mistake! The first time I presented myself at the 'reception' and went up to the counter on the left (that of the Committee of the Regions) instead of the one on the right (that of the Economic and Social Committee), I got the answer: 'No, the European Economic and Social Committee is not here.' Surrealistic discussions about the number of square metres each committee is entitled to recur every year.

This sensitivity can of course also be explained by the use of the building. The luxurious building, named after Jacques Delors, is mainly used for conferences – free for the users – where trade unions are clearly the winners. For them, committees are wonderful conference rooms with all the luxury and translation options available in the European quarter of Brussels.

Yes, it is all well intentioned, but I really do not see the added value of these settings. As chief of staff to the President of the European Economic and Social Committee, we launched the action 'The Wind of Change', inspired by the title of the song by Scorpions. However, the resistance to change is so great and the acquired rights so extensive that any proposal is nipped in the bud. To illustrate: why in the internet era do 350 people have to physically move from their home countries every month to press the 'yes', 'no' or 'abstain' button on the voting box? Not only is this neither economically nor ecologically responsible, but it cannot even be spoken about, because if it were, the house of cards and the cost-reimbursement structure would collapse in an instant.

Additionally, other things have changed since 1957: thousands of lobby groups turn directly to the Commission to make their views known. Where the EESC used to have some added value, that is no longer the case. I see only one solution: abolish those institutions. I do not think anyone, other than the officials and members involved, would take to the streets to protest against such closure. Is that not proof enough?

Those who think less radically could integrate this advisory function into the European Parliament, preferably by reducing staff. It would already be a worthwhile saving.

3.8. SOME ANECDOTES TO ILLUSTRATE

The critical reader might argue that I am exaggerating or regard it as a frustration of the difficulty of reform I have encountered as a private secretary. Reform is always difficult. However, I am a believer in the idea: it was impossible, but nobody told me that.[34] Jean Monnet also voices this same idea when he states in his memoirs: 'can one say that a necessary action is impossible until one has tried it?'[35]

When, as secretary-general in Flanders, I announced on my first day of work that I wanted to abolish the time clock immediately, by midday posters had been put up by the trade unions in all Flemish administrations with the slogan 'Away with Aernoudt'. I had not even signed my contract at the time. But after four months of negotiations and with the promise that those who wished to continue to use the time clock were allowed to do so, I had an agreement. A year later, hardly anyone is using the time clock anymore and many administrations would later follow my example. Not a single ex-colleague dared to refer to the pioneer of that action, who had in the meantime been fired for citing the misuse of taxpayers' money on cabinets.[36]

I only mention this to illustrate the statement that reforming is a natural habit of mine. The then chairman of the EESC, Henri Malosse, a Corsican, was more than happy with the reform. We would give the Committee a new role with a new mission statement. We would stop writing opinions that no one reads and carry out concrete projects and evaluations and launched citizens' initiatives. The bureau – that is the name of the 40-person decision-making body (that of the Committee of the Regions has 63 members), which we called the politburo internally – agreed with our proposal. Apparently, however, they did not understand what they were voting for, because when we wanted to put that decision into practice, protests arose. My chairman was threatened with impeachment, but when we pointed out that this was not provided for in the Internal Rules, a committee was immediately set up to reform those Internal Rules. That again involved many meetings – too many candidates to be members of that committee. But eventually it was determined that there was no consensus and, moreover, the procedures did not allow for the Internal

---

34 This thought is often assigned to Che Guevara, Marc Twain or Winston Churchill.

35 J. Monnet, *Mémoires*, Fayard, 1976: 'Peut-on dire qu'une action nécessaire est impossible aussi longtemps qu'on ne l'a pas essayé ?'

36 The labour court ruled against the government and the responsible minister had to resign.

Rules to be voted on in time. Once approved, the mandate of my president – and therefore mine – would already be over. The Internal Rules would therefore only apply to future presidents, something the successors would rather not have seen. The entire exercise was then stopped. I requested the expenses of daily allowances and plane tickets that this mess had cost from the administration, but it was apparently impossible to calculate.

That incident paralysed my chairman's mandate and started an internal boycott. During the Maidan crisis, the chairman brought in a privileged witness to speak in the plenary session: Viktor Andrijovych Yushchenko, former president of Ukraine and victim of poisoning that left his face disfigured. Incidentally, inviting leading speakers was part of our new mission statement in order to extract the members from their cocoon of the Schuman bubble. Valéry Giscard d'Estaing, Nicolas Hulot and Yves Leterme had already come to speak in that context. The politburo that took place just before the plenary session protested. Yushchenko was allowed to come, but he was not allowed to speak. It was too controversial. This also marked the end of perestroika in the Committee. From now on, everything would once again be done behind closed doors and with a clear agenda: reading opinions, voting on opinions and applauding the rapporteur. And then sending the opinions, in 24 languages, to the Commission.

All in all, I worked for the Commission for about twenty years, mostly on economic issues, and I never once read an opinion from the Committee. However, the Committee's opinions are probably the most expensive ones on the market. The Committee has a budget of €130 million for operating costs. Based on 170 opinions, this works out at €750,000 per opinion or €64,000 per page – a price that reputable consultancy firms can only dream of.

And since working in the committees is slightly less prestigious and less interesting in content than working for the Commission, the committees have a hard time recruiting officials. In order to encourage officials to move from the Commission to the committees, a number of attractive incentives have been developed. For example, there is no work on Friday afternoons. Promotion is also much faster. And the desks are bigger.

On this point, my president made a serious mistake when he proposed to place the members in the prestigious main building (the Jacques Delors building) and the officials in the annex. After all, the Committee is made up of members and not officials. This was of course beyond the pale for the officials of the civil service, who invoked all kinds of procedures and budgetary constraints to boycott the move – successfully, as it turned out: it is now the other way around. The world turned upside down. Procedures are, by definition, strong in an administration, but at the same time the administration can also be the victim of them. Indeed, procedures can often mean that the administration loses its link with reality. To give an example, one of the Committee's former chairmen had died. Coincidentally, there was a plenary session the next day. So, I asked the administration to provide me with a book of condolence. This was of course beyond the scope of the procedures, because a purchase could only be made by organizing a limited tender, which would take a few days. Hilarious! I then asked my personal assistant to buy a book of condolence in the shop next door and paid for it myself.

3.9. RELATIONSHIP BETWEEN THE OFFICIALS AND THE 'ELECTED' MEMBERS

This brings me to the difficult relationship between civil servants and 'elected' members. Unlike the European Parliament, the members of the committees are not actually elected, but rather appointed by their 'parent organizations'. It is the trade unions, employers' organizations and lobby groups that appoint their representatives to 'sit' on the committees. Often, as discussed, they are veterans. Let us take the example of the employers' organizations (group I) in the Economic and Social Committee. They are usually former presidents of Chambers of Commerce or other employers' organizations, including employees of those organizations. The employers are therefore represented by employees. There are hardly any entrepreneurs among the 123 members who represent the entrepreneurial voice. It reminds me of one of my favourite philosophers, Jacques Derrida, who argued that representation (*ré-présentation*) actually refers to the absence of those who should be there.[37]

The relationship between the appointed representatives and the officials is particularly difficult. Let us again take the Economic and Social Committee: 720 officials – not including translation services – or two officials per member. The members come and go (two-and-a-half-year mandates); the civil servants remain.

Officials have exactly the same statute as Commission officials, which, as discussed above, is rather generous. Members receive their daily and expense allowances. The members must therefore keep their expense

[37] J. Derrida, *La différance [The differance]*, Seuil, 1974.

reports for the administration and also demonstrate their presence. The latter is done by signing the attendance register at the entrance of the meeting rooms. Members are also entitled to a so-called 'white day' referring to a day squeezed between two meeting days. Indeed, if a member has a meeting on Tuesday and another on Thursday, it is assumed that the member would also be in Brussels on the Wednesday, even without a meeting, and that entitles him to a daily allowance. Yes, all that was put into regulations and approved by the politburo.

In contrast, officials who are required to audit members are paid much more generously, and are not required to demonstrate attendance or to keep receipts. However, the committees should really be about the members. For example, the chairmen of the committees receive, in addition to his daily allowances and expenses, a one-off sum of €30,000 per year (the chairman's bonus). The highest-ranking official – the secretary-general – is an AD16 and therefore earns €21,000 per month. However, the fate of the secretary-general and the appointment of other directors is decided by the politburo. The career of senior officials thus depends mainly on the goodwill they can obtain from the members.

This relationship is thus quite ambiguous and is coloured by something between jealousy and flattery. That is the perfect condition for sexual harassment. This not only leads to personal trauma, but also to absenteeism due to illness and to a drop in productivity. The Committee on Budgetary Control (COCOBU) found the material damage caused by the various cases that had arisen in the European Parliament, the committees and the European Court of Auditors so serious that it decided to organize a workshop on the financial consequences of harassment in the European institutions.

As a result, a zero-tolerance policy towards cases of harassment was introduced. The European Court of Justice has already several times ordered the European Parliament and the European Investment Bank to pay damages to employees who have been victims of moral harassment. Not very reassuring.

But in the European Economic and Social Committee the intimidation conditions are worse. The European Court has already pointed out that 'the management style does not correspond to the administrative culture of European public service'.[38] Among other things, mention was made of obliging civil servants to work during their maternity leave. The Court

[38] Case F-50/15 *FS v EESC*, Court report of 12 May 2016.

therefore invited the administration to inform members about the essential principles of European culture.

The problems are also reflected in the number of annual cases of intimidation: up to 25 per year for an institution with 700 officials is a lot. 'The cases of harassment in the committee not only damage the reputation of the institution, the committee members and officials, but also cause psychological damage to the victims,' said Madi Sharma, a British former member of the Committee.[39] It costs the Committee €55,000 per year to defend members and officials, processes that are invariably lost … by the Committee.[40] Indeed, a #MeToo movement is urgently needed in the European institutions. Incidentally, cases of sexual harassment are rife and many files end up at the offices of OLAF (the anti-fraud service) and some even at the offices of the Belgian judiciary. Parliament hated it so much that in 2022, for the first time in history, it refused to approve the Committee's budget. And the chairman-to-be – it is customary for the chairman of the group to be chaired to also become Committee chairman – had to reluctantly put his chairmanship ambitions aside.

4. THE CIVILIAN GAP

The gap between Europe and its citizens exists in the minds of the people.

The Gap
Esther de Lange and Ivo Belet[41]

The Eurocracy seen as an elite caste that has lost touch with reality, a flood of law pouring out over the heads of its citizens and concocted by the Schuman roundabout bubble and national and regional politicians who use Europe as a scapegoat are the perfect ingredients to engender citizen apathy.

The texts of the European institutions are worse than a doctor's report. They are laced with Eurocrat jargon and although they are translated into all languages, they remain unintelligible to many. Jean Monnet's grandson told me that his grandfather used to have documents from the

39 https://m.publico.es/sociedad/2068749/una-docena-de-denuncias-y-silencio-por-respuesta-el-acoso-laboral-golpea-al-comite-economico-y-social-europeo.

40 'Violence against women and sexual harassment', *EP Magazine*, November 2018.

41 I. Belet and E. De Langhe, *De kloof, Is Europa nog van ons [The gap, is Europe still ours]*, Lannoo, 2017.

administration read by his driver. If the driver did not understand them, Monnet sent them back. Yes, we should do that in Europe too.

4.1. REFERENDUM CULTURE?

Citizens expressed their aversion to the European project whenever they had the chance. As mentioned, only half of Europeans still turn up for European elections, and only one-third in the UK. In referendums, European citizens have repeatedly spoken out against Europe, against the new constitution (France and the Netherlands), against the treaty with Ukraine (the Netherlands), and against accession (Norway and, twice, Switzerland).

We always try to circumvent the will of the people with state-of-the-art legal and political technology. When the Danes voted in a referendum against the Maastricht Treaty that created a genuine European Union, Denmark only joined the new EU structures after it had negotiated exceptional measures to stay out of the eurozone and cooperation in justice and home affairs. The Danish krone was not in danger. Technically, it was pegged to the euro.

The Nice Reform Treaty, with new powers for the EU, was first rejected by the Irish in 2001, but after a number of adjustments they gave it the green light the following year.

When the French and Dutch rejected the constitution, by 54% and 61% respectively, all other referendums on the EU constitution in Britain and Ireland, among others, were cancelled and the treaty had to be renegotiated. The same constitution was later approved, subject to some cosmetic interventions, without again consulting the population. The only country where this has happened – because it is constitutionally required there – is Ireland. The cosmetic version of the constitution, now called the Lisbon Reform Treaty, was initially rejected by the Irish in 2008 with 53%, but in a second referendum, a year later and after a few adjustments, it was passed with 67%.

A referendum on an exit is of course rather difficult to avoid. The demand for a second referendum on the same subject, what the group around Tony Blair and others wanted for Brexit, actually sends the message that the British had not understood what they had voted for. And even if that were the case, it would seem difficult to give the population a second chance.

Incidentally, the British had actually already voted on a possible Brexit, namely in 1975, two years after accession. It was an election promise from

Labour leader Harold Wilson, who won the election because he promised to organize a referendum on the United Kingdom's European membership. According to the polls, a first Brexit was already imminent. Even then the polls were wrong. 67% of Britons chose Europe. The country was then in a deep economic and social crisis and the British had put their hopes in Europe.

Besides, a second chance does not always lead to a turnaround, as the example of the Irish mentioned above might suggest. In Norway there were no less than 23 years – a complete generational change – between the first referendum (1972) and the second (1995), but the result remained the same. Nobody knows – polls are still taken seriously by few people – whether a second referendum would have produced an anti-Brexit result.

Brexit is the first EU exit. Greater London, Scotland and Northern Ireland were against it, so it was basically the choice of the regions of Midlands, Northern England and Wales to leave the EU. However, it was not the first time that a region had left. In 1985, 35 years ago, the island of Greenland, an autonomous area within Denmark, withdrew from the EU after, yes, a referendum.

The question, of course, is whether a referendum is the right tool for deciding whether or not a country should remain in the Union or whether or not to adopt a constitution. Who has ever read the constitution? Copies of the constitution were distributed in the streets at the time of the referendum in France. That is ridiculous. Would the euro ever have come about on the basis of a referendum?

Most European countries do not have a referendum culture, with the exception of Switzerland, which is not part of the Union, and I do not see it joining in the long term. Even membership of the European Economic Area is not an option for it, unlike the other former members of the European Free Trade Area.

4.2. THE VOICE OF THE CITIZEN

Citizens can not only vote in the five-yearly elections for Members of the European Parliament or possibly through referenda, but can also take matters into their own hands. After all, the citizens' initiative has existed since the Treaty of Lisbon. Citizens can take the initiative to put a certain topic on the European agenda if they can have a petition signed by at least one million citizens. The Committee is not obliged to put the subject on the agenda, but is 'encouraged' to do so, in diplomatic parlance.

These initiatives usually relate to subjects that directly affect citizens. For example, an initiative was launched to abolish roaming charges in Europe, which the Commission converted into a regulation before the initiative came to an end. This means EU citizens travelling within the EU can use their mobile phones to make calls, send text messages and access the internet at the same price as in their home country, making a significant difference to their phone bills and especially to the bills of travellers, and to Erasmus students. After all, surfing and WhatsApping is now possible from abroad without additional costs – a world of difference.

Box 2. Free tap water

The citizens' initiative Right2Water was able to convince 1.6 million European citizens, thus far more than the required million. As a result, the Commission adapted the Water Directive by adding an article that every Member State must ensure as much as possible that citizens, both indoors and outdoors, have free access to drinking water. The Commission also urged the hospitality industry to offer a *carafe d'eau* free of charge to their customers, as is customary in countries such as France. The sector responded by stating that serving the water, especially in a country with a high labour cost burden, is not free. Just ask for a *carafe d'eau* in Belgium and you will see that it rarely works. Nevertheless, I think it is good that the Commission encourages and does not impose. I did the test myself, just outside the European Union, in a pizzeria in Geneva. 'Can I get a *carafe d'eau*?' 'No, we don't offer that, at least not for free.' I still ordered my *carafe d'eau*, for which I paid 3.50 CHF. Perhaps the Swiss pragmatism model can be found here too. After all, free means that someone other than the user pays the bill.

4.3. WHY IS THERE A GAP WITH THE CITIZEN?

The question that naturally arises is whether there is such a thing as European identity. If the Briton is asked whether he feels British or European, we know the answer; at least of the majority. If you ask the Fleming whether he feels Belgian or Flemish, we invariably get a majority that opts for the Flemish identity. Ask a Breton or a Corsican if he or she feels regional, French or European and we know the answer. The same applies if a Frisian is asked whether his or her identity is regional, national or European. But actually, the question is wrong. After all, we are complex beings with overlapping, intertwined identities.

The European identity is therefore an overlapping – and not an overarching – identity. We are all Belgian, Flemish, British, Spanish, etc., but also European. Religious or not, we are all children of the Judeo-Christian culture and at the same time children of the Enlightenment.

The idea is often attributed to Monnet that if he started over, he would start with the culture. As a philosopher, I do not agree at all. As shown before, the genesis of the European Union is one of economic cooperation, as it was clearly demonstrated there that it was a win–win relationship. In culture, exchange can be enriching – I am a big fan of the Erasmus programme – but that cannot provide a sustainable basis for cooperation. The fact that there is such a thing as a European hymn – *lle Menschen werden Brüder* (All Men Will Become Brothers) by Ludwig von Beethoven, by the way chosen by Coudenhove-Kalergi – a European flag and European symbols is nice, but that is not a sufficient basis for building a real 'Community between European citizens'.

The citizen must therefore benefit from Europe. That is precisely why Europe must always ask in its policy what the impact is on the life and quality of life of its citizens. We must not lose sight of the fact that there is a perception problem. When Nigel Farage states, on the eve of Brexit, that the British will gain £350 million for the NHS if they leave the Union, that sounds credible. The fact that he says the day after Brexit that his figures are not correct is, unfortunately, a *fait diver*. Yes, the media also have a social responsibility. Europe is too often used as a scapegoat for everything that goes wrong. When a budget goes off track, one does not point to the responsibility of the politicians who did deficit spending, but instead points the finger at Europe for imposing austerity measures.

The perception of overpaid bureaucrats enacting laws and regulations that complicate the life of the 'ordinary citizen' only widens the gap with the citizen. The turnout figures discussed above in European Parliament elections can be regarded as a barometer in this regard. Brexit, ironically, brought some change here and, contradictorily enough, formed the basis for a new impetus for Europe.

CHAPTER 2
EUROPE: THE FOUR SCENARIOS

Europe,
Where's the narrative?

Rudy Aernoudt

The question is: how should we proceed now? Can Europe just muddle on now that the momentum has ebbed? Or should we just stop, as has happened with a lot of past integration efforts throughout the world? Or should we breathe new life into Europe and if so, how? Let us take a closer look at four possible scenarios.

1. EURO-MADNESS

Europe is the future. Member States are the past. This is how we could summarize this scenario. All tasks should be transferred to the supranational level as much as possible. European taxes, direct European elections, a European army – these are just a few of the many possibilities.

Guy Verhofstadt, former leader of the ALDE (liberals) group in the European Parliament, is an adoptee of this philosophy. He advocates a United States of Europe with a European diplomatic corps, a European army and a genuine European government.[42] Valéry Giscard d'Estaing and Helmut Schmidt also have far-reaching proposals that make Europe a fully integrated monetary, budgetary and fiscal zone.[43] This philosophy is based on the idea that what is done at European level is done better.

---

42 G. Verhofstadt, *De Verenigde Staten van Europa [The United States of Europe]*, Houtekiet, 2005.

43 V. Giscard d'Estaing and H. Smidt, *Europa, la Dernière chance de l'Europe [Europa, the Last chance for Europe]*, XO, 2014.

The gap with the citizens makes such an approach unfeasible; that is not realpolitik. Citizens already believe that everything is decided in Brussels. Entrusting yet more powers to the Schuman bubble would only exacerbate those problems and lead to further mistrust in the European construction.

The Euro-madness approach is not only unfeasible, but also undesirable. After all, from the earlier points it may be concluded that Europe is not a nirvana. It does not make sense to want to do everything on a supranational level.

Besides, the European construction is a gradual process, not one that aims to bring everything up to the European level, gradually eroding the powers at national and regional level. It only makes sense to bring a certain domain wholly or partly to the European level if there is real added value in doing so. Nor was it ever the intention of the fathers of Europe to create a kind of Moscow in Brussels.

Incidentally, the concept of 'the United States of' does not seem attractive to me as a model for Europe. In this I join the Europhobes, who see the United States of Europe as a disaster.[44]

2. EUROPHOBIA

This brings us to the other end of the spectrum: the Europhobes. Europe is the source of all evil. How good would life be if we could get rid of the Brussels juggernaut? This is how we could summarize their belief.

They had their first success with Brexit. 'We want our country back,' they said, echoing the Thatcherian thought in unison. The British economy would be so much better without the expensive membership of the European Union. After all, the refugee problem is the fault of Brussels bureaucrats. The then President of the European Council, Herman Van Rompuy, according to Nigel Farage, has the charisma of a mop, which caused much amusement among the audience. When I debated the issue with Farage and discussed the impact on the economy, he laughed at it. The British knew better how to conduct economic policy than the Eurocrats, he said.[45]

---

44 V. Van der Sterren, 'De Verenigde Staten van Europa: een ramp' ['The United States of Europe: a disaster'], in W. Van Rooy et al, *Europa Wankelt [Europe Falters]*, Uitgeverij van Halewyck, 2012.

45 See LVSV, Nigel Farage versus Rudy Aernoudt: A new Europe in sight?, https://alchetron.com/Rudy-Aernoudt.

In the meantime, we know better. The pound crashed after Brexit. The British economy was predicted to contract by 8% with a hard Brexit and by 3% with a soft Brexit. And most of the regulations that Europe adopted along with the British will continue to be respected by the British.

The chaos surrounding Brexit and the economic impact made the voices of other Brexiteers more muted. But the most extreme continued to advocate exit from the Union or at least from the monetary union.

Marine Le Pen, unhampered by knowledge of the matter, proposed to stop using the euro and advocated a return to the French franc. When asked about the impact on companies, her answer during the presidential debate was enlightening: companies would continue to work in euros, make payments and issue receipts in euros, but employees would only work in French francs. That would be a fun affair, over in France.

In the Netherlands, too, some have gone wild. Wilders, intending to prove his point, ordered a study from the Eurosceptical think-tank Lombard Street Research, which of course concluded that the costs for the Netherlands in leaving the eurozone would be recouped in two years. So, a good investment. The dream of a Nexit, however, was shelved, at least by most Dutch people, when the dire impact of Brexit became clear.

To take another example, Johan Van Overtveldt, currently an MEP, gave a lecture in the European Parliament in which he argued for the end of the euro and of the monetary union.[46] He advocated a return to national currencies, echoing Marine Le Pen's vision. Specifically, he proposed that Germany, the Netherlands, Finland and Austria should leave the currency union. Three years later, he became a member of the right-wing Flemish party and became federal minister of finance, and hence a member of the Eurogroup, trying to defend the euro. A constant in politics: what one says is often not determined by what one thinks, but by what position one holds. By analogy, I myself was for a long period – too long – chief of staff to a federal Belgian minister who advocated the re-federalization of foreign trade when she was federal minister, and emerged as a staunch regionalist who opposed federal foreign trade missions when she became a regional minister.

What is striking is that many Europhobes often also have other phobias, including towards migrants or towards members of the LGBTQIA+ community. The parties against Europe are often extremist parties, mostly

---

46 J. Van Overtveldt, 'The end of the euro', speech in the European Parliament in 2011 based on his book with the same title. As finance minister, he had to resign as a result of the Migration Pact and later became a Member of the European Parliament again.

from the right, but also from the left. The attitude of 'our own people first' is apparently at odds with the idea of Europe. Characteristic of these parties is also the demagogic language that rarely passes a fact check. Examples are legion.

Some Europhobes even go so far as to compare the European idea of unification with the unification projects of the Nazis or their allies. John Laughland, a British Eurosceptic conservative and director of the European Foundation, concludes his article with the proverbial title 'Fascists and Federalists' as follows: 'There is an overlap between the Nazi and pro-European streams of thought whose antecedents reach into the European intellectual and geopolitical history of the outbreak of the Second World War'.[47]

Finally, what is also striking is the fact that those parties that are against Europe are doing everything they can to claim their seats in the European Parliament and the committees. They are against it, but apparently want to stay on the payroll.

Europhobes have learned no lessons from history. They are folded in on themselves and have no future whatsoever. All they can do is damage the European process, but unfortunately they do not have to pay for the damage they themselves provoked. It is the average Brit, who believed the story of Farage and Co., who is presented with the bill now. This is in stark contrast to Nigel Farage himself, who continued to be paid from Europe for years after the Brexit referendum.

3. STATUS QUO

Is everything then rose-scented and moonshine? No, a procession of Echternach in which an army of Eurocrats legitimizes itself with a flood of law (everywhere) that descends on the countries and regions from above, as something transcendental or even divine, is not a sustainable option. A Europe that drags itself from one crisis to another, a Europe without a president, but with a president of the Commission, a president of the Council of the European Union, a rotating president of the European Council, you name it – how can such a thing continue to exist? Former

47 J. Laighland, 'Fascisten en federalisten' ['Fascists and Federalists'] in W. Van Rooy et al., *Europa Wankelt [Europe Falters]*, Uitgeverij van Halewyck, 2012.

United States Secretary of State Harry Kissinger's question, 'If I want to speak to Europe, who should I call?' is still very relevant. And Erdogan understood this too when he forced the two presidents to perform musical chairs, with haunting images unworthy of a president of the Council of the European Union.

This is a Europe where citizens increasingly drop out because the story becomes unintelligible, or even more so, where there is no more story. Many speeches about Europe start with history, with the World Wars, but that is no longer useful to our young people. War is something from the history books or from distant lands. How can such a story make today's young people enthusiastic about Europe?

We need to learn from Europe what really has an impact on European life. And in doing so, we must be careful of the little stories that repeatedly cast Europe in a bad light. For example, a Europe that wants to determine how much water can be used to flush the toilet and that pays consultants €80,000 to map the European sanitation mentality; a Europe that considered banning restaurant owners from using olive oil carafes several times – you name it.

We should focus on the European (and not on his toilet). Erasmus, for example, is a fantastic project. Unfortunately, I was born just too early to enjoy it, but I think it is the most beautiful success in Europe. I also think the euro is such a beautiful story. The euro makes Europe feel every moment of the day. It makes Europe alive. It is undoubtedly an important reason that explains why Europhobes also often target the euro and argue for the return to national currencies. After all, they are pocket-sized national identities.

The question, of course, is: what is the narrative today? What is the story that makes Europeans think European and act European? The zeal for law, the Eurocracy, the Brussels ivory tower do not provide a sufficient answer to that question. Muddling through is not an option.

4. A PRAGMATIC APPROACH

The European story is too unique to fall into extreme dogmas – Euromadness or Europhobia. The story is also too good to gradually fade away or evaporate for lack of new impetus.

The alternative to a dogmatic approach is a pragmatic approach, in which the question is asked for each domain whether we do things better together, or whether we are better off doing things on our own; in other words, whether we are doing something better at European, national or regional level.

To create this, we do not even have to reinvent the wheel. After all, there is a clear principle, namely the principle of subsidiarity, with which we can map out what we are doing better at European level based on qualitative and quantitative indicators for each policy area.

I would go even further and say that, when there is doubt, we should choose the lowest possible level of government. In this way, we return to the basic principle that applied when Europe was founded: opt for cooperation in those areas that are strategically important for Europe and where European cooperation offers clear added value. In other words, the question we have to ask ourselves is: what are the coal and steel industries of today?

Why would such a pragmatic approach be politically feasible? As sad as I think Brexit is for the United Kingdom and for the European Union, we should consider this event a unique opportunity for Europe. We have to be able to differentiate between an obstacle and an opportunity and try to turn both in our favour, Machiavelli said. Well, Brexit is one such obstacle that harbours an opportunity.

First and foremost, Brexit makes it clear to other countries that a European referendum should not be used to settle internal problems. Brexit has more than clearly demonstrated the enormous difficulties associated with leaving the European Union and the pernicious impact on a country's economy. This did not even happen in a country that belonged to the monetary union or the Schengen zone. This encourages other countries where the idea of exit is also sometimes suggested to think more pragmatically and less dogmatically.

More importantly, countries that often automatically sided with the UK's positions must now devise a different strategy. We often saw in the past that the United Kingdom and a few small countries such as the Netherlands, Denmark and Sweden could together ensure that no qualified majority could be found. In order to exert influence in the European Union now, these countries must look for new allies. The Netherlands, for example, establishes contact with Spain, France and the Baltic states and no longer has its back turned to Berlin.

Countries such as Sweden and Denmark, which often seamlessly aligned themselves with the British stance, have had to switch sides. According to the Swedish think tank Sieps, Sweden only really became a member of the European Union after Brexit. 'We saw everything through the British eyes,' the think tank concludes, 'but the last thing Sweden and Denmark want is an exit.'[48] And countries like the Czech Republic, Malta and Ireland, who are not particularly keen of the banking union, now want an observer status in it.

It is clear that Brexit has made the 27 remaining countries become more European. After all, the British attitude of reluctance was often an excuse that other countries used to hide behind.[49] This applies not only to the Member States, but also to Europeans, who are increasingly positive about Europe in the Eurobarometer. Ex post, Brexit could well be the new engine of European construction. It would be a shame to let such a crisis go untapped. Brexit is the ideal impetus for a new Europe, a Europe that does not want to be dictatorial or a bureaucrat-led project, but a Europe of the citizens, a Europe where pragmatism triumphs and dogmatism is suppressed. So, time for a new impetus, time for a pragmatic Europe.

48 'Brexit – Implications for the EU and Sweden', Swedish Institute of for European Policy Studies (SIEPS), Stockholm, June 2017, https://sieps.se/contentassets/3f0831dcf51f47289872e1eff06201e5/brexit_english.pdf?.

49 M. Calligaro and E. Cardère, *Les Compromis [Compromises]*, Payot-rivages, 2020.

CHAPTER 3
EUROPE: THE NEW IMPETUS

Where focus goes, energy flows.

Tony Robbins
Twitter, 14 May 2020

How do you build a pragmatic Europe? Well, as with any company in crisis, Europe must return to its core activity, which is to do that what improves the quality of life of citizens, and only where they do better than a lower administrative level. In doing so, Europe must discard ballast, develop a lean and mean structure and pursue its own value model, instead of wanting to outperform other continents.

1. END OF THE JUGGERNAUT

Europe and the European institutions are victims of the inflation of bureaucracy, as the German sociologist Max Weber called this. An army of 50,000 officials should keep Europe on the right track. The bureaucracy has become its own community, its own 'bubble', with its own laws and its own privileges.

Some argue that this monster administration is the price of democracy. I think it is exactly the opposite. Spread over more than 50 buildings in Brussels and present in most countries of the world, the juggernaut is rather a source of alienation. Eurocrats usually write notes to each other, meet among themselves or inter-institutionally, as it is called. It is a closed cocoon that closes itself off from the citizen.

By analogy with large companies that are losing weight, Europe must also go on a diet. To do this there are many obstacles, both political and administrative.

1.1. THE ELECTED REPRESENTATIVES: OBSTACLES OF A POLITICAL NATURE

The Commission is a European body. That means that the Commission and its members work for Europe and not for their country. It is therefore pointless for Member States to want their country to have a commissioner. This does not make sense. Moreover, the commissioner is given a certain competence. How can he or she work for the 'motherland'? Didier Reynders, for example, is a Justice Commissioner. That is all well and good, but what is in it for Belgium, his country of origin? And when a country enters or leaves the Union, a new commissioner has to be appointed or withdrawn. Due to the Brexit referendum, Jonathon Hill, who held the important portfolio of the banking union, resigned and was replaced by Julian King, who stayed on as UK commissioner until the referendum was translated into a real exit, three and a half years later, with the portfolio of security. A ridiculous circus. This shows that we need to put an end to the idea that each country needs a commissioner. This is against the idea of a real Europe.

And just as with members of the European Parliament, the appointment of commissioners is often led by criteria that go beyond competence. To illustrate, Karel De Gucht became Commissioner of Foreign Trade, a prestigious post but in fact a sanction imposed on him by the Belgian Prime Minister at that time, Guy Verhofstadt, following a conflict of views about migrant voting rights. 'Karel, if you don't adjust your point of view, I'll send you to the Commission.' That is what happened. In the meantime, Verhofstadt became, like so many, after his prime ministerial mandate, a Member of the European Parliament. The most striking example in European history is that of Jacques Delors, who was sent to Brussels as a consolation prize after failing to become Prime Minister in France – Mitterrand preferred the younger Laurent Fabius – and turned out to be one of the best Commission Presidents ever.

If we accept that not every Member State has a commissioner, we can slim down the top of the Commission. Incidentally, how can you run a company with 27 board members who all have to be accountable to their government? Following the example of the United Nations, we could agree on a rotation principle whereby countries always skip a turn. That would halve the number of commissioners.

Their number is a problem not only because it entails many costs, but also because, generally, the field of competence of each commissioner is so limited that one can quickly end up in the domain of another commissioner – whether overlapping or not – with all the sensitivities linked to this. It would therefore also be much more efficient to reduce the number of commissioners. It would be a sign of statesmanship if the European Council of Ministers were ever to implement such a decision.

What is true for the Commission is, of course, even more so for institutions such as the Court of Auditors or the European Court of Justice. Why should all countries have a member there? There is really no reason for this.

As far as Parliament is concerned, it makes no sense to bring together a general assembly of more than 700 members. Have you ever attended such a plenary session? Most MEPs are there without bringing any added value. Based on the philosophy that if your presence does not add value, your absence will not make a difference, we can ask whether we really would have less democracy if we halved the number of members. The only problem would be that a lot of discarded politicians would no longer have a Strasbourg exit. *Et alors?*

Their suitcases with files usually stand unopened in the corridors of Strasbourg. The travelling circus that should symbolize the democratic content of Europe in fact makes itself endlessly ridiculous. Since Parliament is an example of democracy and takes decisions by majority, I am in favour of a vote that determines where Parliament is located. Brussels or Strasbourg? In today's digital age, it would be no problem at all for the Parliament to be located in Strasbourg. The occasional need for a few commissioners or Eurocrats to travel to Strasbourg would be a significant time- and cost-saving improvement compared to the current situation.

And then the committees. Yes, consultation is important. Consulting the regions about areas that concern them is helpful. That trade unions and employers also have their say – why not? But do we need separate institutions for this? There are already sufficient resources to consult them. Every time the Commission launches a new proposal, a public consultation is launched. Thousands of Europeans express their opinion in this way. Regions, employers, employees and other lobby groups also let the Commission know in this way what they think of a proposal and what they would change. Some even argue that the Commission has become easy prey for consultants and lobbyists, but that is another story.[50]

Anyway, these direct stakeholder consultations – as they are called in Euro-jargon – are an immense success, meaning that the added value of the consultation committees is close to zero. Get rid of those costly, useless committees.

---

50 H. Malosse, in *Le Crépuscule des bureaucrates, chronique de la fin de l'Union européenne [The Twilight of the Bureaucrats, chronicling the end of the European Union]*, Editions Paliot, 2020.

1.2. THE EUROCRATS: OBSTACLES OF AN ADMINISTRATIVE NATURE

Then we have the bureaucracy. Since the majority have been appointed for life and have not been elected and therefore do not have to be re-elected, this is a different matter. You cannot just fire the Eurocrats, except for some very exceptional cases of professional misconduct.

But if Europe focuses on the essentials, it does not need a very hierarchical structured team with a lot of management levels. Here I would propose a reduction. The Commission's trade unions are calling for more recruitment as the army is getting old, but I would instead suggest taking advantage of that unique opportunity. Make a plan in which three Eurocrats who have earned a rest are replaced by one person, so that the juggernaut is gradually reduced in function of the core tasks. This also means that some tasks will be divested, not by transferring them to one of the many agencies – there is also proliferation there – but by simply abolishing certain tasks. In other words, by not doing some things anymore.

2. WHAT EUROPE SHOULD NOT DO ANYMORE

Europe must give impetus to the Member States, but does it have to set up and finance micro-projects around the world to do this? Should Europe manage grants for businesses? Should Europe decide how crooked a banana or cucumber should be?

Before Europe gets involved in a domain, three tests should be carried out beforehand: the project should have a clear European dimension, harmonization should not be an objective and symbolic files should be avoided.

2.1. EUROPEAN DIMENSION

Europe should only be involved in areas with a clear European dimension. Although this may seem obvious a priori, it is not always the case. For example, what is the European added value of financing training? It exists if there is a European dimension, but most projects, for example those financed by the European Social Fund, have no added value at European level. I think there should be training to orient people in the digital world and, yes, I am in favour of dual learning, just to name two examples, but why on earth should such initiatives be financed by Europe? Why should Europe fund national and regional employment agencies? That is not necessary. Thousands of Eurocrats are engaged in the research, analysis and evaluation of such projects without any European added value. Setting up thousands of projects to recover part of the contribution is a bureaucratic, pointless undertaking.

To take another example: the European Globalization Fund. Employees who have become unemployed as a result of an economic crisis or a changing market due to globalization can call on this fund to help them reintegrate into the labour market. Of course, I am not against that, but again: why at the European level? Incidentally, the support is one-off and specifically aimed at individual employees. In concrete terms, the European Globalization Fund thus finances, among other things, education and training, retraining, outplacement, guidance when starting your own business and follow-up in the search for new work. The European Globalization Fund provides up to 50% of the costs of reintegrating employees into the labour market. The remaining costs are covered by national, regional or private funds. The support of the Globalization Fund is always additional: it complements actions by Member States at national, regional and local level and measures taken by companies under national law or collective agreements. Let us leave that to the Member States at national or regional level depending on the governance structure of each country.

As yet another example, the European Asylum, Migration and Integration Fund is a financial instrument of the European Commission aimed at more efficient management of migratory flows and the strengthening and development of a common approach to asylum, migration and integration. The resources are allocated as a priority to closing the employment gap, improving access to public services and setting up actions for certain subgroups (women, young people, etc.). All these actions specifically target persons without EU nationality (third-country nationals). In addition to the calls that the Member States prepare themselves, the European Commission is also launching its own calls in the context of Union Actions. There is no European story and no European added value.

These three examples are sufficient to show that Europe should withdraw from all actions that do not have a European dimension. Europe should only intervene if several countries are involved.

Imagine an Erasmus for entrepreneurs: starting entrepreneurs can do a training internship for six months in a similar company abroad. This is a concrete programme with a clear European dimension. The same reasoning applies to companies. Europe should only provide support if there is a European dimension. The aforementioned former JEV programme that supported companies to set up joint ventures with companies from another European Union country was a good way to teach companies to work together across national borders. When it turned out that companies were mature enough to do so without government support, the programme was abolished. That too is important.

If we were to screen all of Europe's programmes for their European dimension, many domains would be destroyed and Eurocrats could focus on projects where Europe really makes a difference. The army of the Eurocrats could downsize considerably.

2.2. HARMONIZATION DRIFT

In addition, Europe must curb its drive to harmonize. Harmonization is not an end but a means to make the internal market work properly. That does not mean everything has to be equal. The mutual recognition procedure seems to me to be more logical.

In concrete terms, this means that Europe should no longer prioritize the harmonization of products. The curvature of cucumbers or bananas or the number of litres of water that the toilet bowl is allowed to use should no longer be a European competence. However, Europe can set minimum criteria, mainly with regard to health and hygiene, that products must meet if they want to circulate freely across borders.

As another example, salaries, social legislation and tax scales remain the competency of national and regional governments. Only the principle that the applicable law is the law of the place of employment is established. So, not everything has to be harmonized there either.

2.3. SYMBOLIC FILES ARE TO BE AVOIDED

Finally, Europe should not lose time and energy on symbolic files. Symbolic files are usually relatively unimportant files that can get people fired up because of some symbolic value. Just to illustrate, the well-known English Stilton received a protected designation of origin (PDO), but precisely because of this, this exclusive Stilton is no longer produced according to the traditional recipe, because Stilton PDO can only be made with pasteurized milk and industrially prepared rennet – the enzyme chymosin, extracted from yeast – and no longer with raw milk and rennet with enzymes from the abomasum of calves. The Stilton saga was once again diluted by the perception of the Brussels bureaucratic monster with its innumerable, sometimes even conflicting, regulations.

To stay in the world of cheese, the typical cheese of Sardinia, casu marzu – literally 'rotten cheese' – was banned by the European Commission, but after protests, the ban was lifted and the cheese was given the status of guaranteed traditional specialty.

Or take the example of the famous French Camembert de Normandie, made from raw milk. It had an AOC (appéllation d'origine contrôlée). This changed in 2021 with the introduction of a second, pasteurized version of the labelled cheese. This can therefore call itself 'Camembert de Normandie', even without a raw-milk base. Its raw-milk counterpart is since sold as 'Véritable Camembert de Normandie'.

The Belgian cheese Herve also has European origin protection. When the Federal Agency for the Safety of the Food Chain (FASFC) shut down production because traces of listeria were found, there was a great regional commotion and Europe was naturally singled out for blame. However, further investigation revealed that production was fully in accordance with European standards, but that the FASFC had applied its own standards, which were stricter than those of Europe, to shut down the company. Although such decisions are probably very responsible from a health point of view, I do wonder whether such prohibitions do not cause more damage to Europe than they avoid in damage to health. Again, perception is reality.

Box 3. The tampon taxes

The UK's first post-Brexit decision, following the trade deal that came into effect on 1 January 2021, was to abolish VAT on tampons. After all, the EU law stated that the minimum VAT on non-essential luxury products is 5%. Freed from the Brussels yoke, the British were able to abolish this tampon tax. It was a symbolic file. Instead of £3, a pack of tampons now cost £2.85, but the symbolic value was much higher.

Geopolitically, it was also a bonus that the beneficiaries of this measure were women, who had voted overwhelmingly against Brexit, and it was also a nod to Scotland, a pro-European region, which had previously made tampons tax-free. Eurocrats should have the tampon tax in mind before pushing through certain guidelines for health or other considerations.

3. THE CALIMERO COMPLEX

All too often we look at America as the land of milk and honey, the land of pioneers and the entrepreneurial spirit, the country with China hot on its heels in a competition that has long since been abandoned by Europe. This situation is snidely summarized as if Europe was the continent where scientists invent things and publish their results, but see the applications, the real innovation happen in the United States. China is considered the country of imitation. Such clichés are harmful, but they do have a grain of truth. Many articles or commission papers start with an analysis of the divide with the United States. This applies, for example, to most analyses of innovation or venture capital.

However, it also applies to Europe's global strategy. When Jacques Delors became President of the European Commission and was asked about his objective, he replied: 'Be as competitive as the United States and Asia.'[51] That was the driving force behind the internal market and behind monetary union. But even now that is still the case. The Lisbon strategy, for example, dominated the European calendar for the first twenty years of the twenty-first century. This strategy, also known as the Lisbon process, is an action and development plan of and for the European Union that was adopted in the year 2000 and had a duration of ten years. It was continued in its successor, the Europe 2020 strategy.

The starting point of the strategy was the gap with the United States. The gross domestic product per capita – the barometer for the prosperity of a population – was on average 30% lower in Europe than in the United States. One of the reasons was the fact that Europe lagged significantly behind the United States in research investment. In the year 2000, Europe was at the level where the United States was in 1966. A second reason was that many more Americans than Europeans were employed.

Europe therefore had to focus on research and development and get more Europeans into work in order to keep up with the level of prosperity in the United States. This is the core of the Lisbon strategy. The objectives were therefore quantified. After all, objective quantification makes monitoring and reporting on the basis of on-board tables and intermediate reports easier. The objective was to ensure that by 2010 the European Union would become the most competitive and dynamic knowledge-based economy

---

51 F. Ruffing, 'J. Delors, L'homme des Firmes' ['J. Delors, the corporate man'], in *Le fakir n°(40) février – mars* 2009.

in the world, including through a 70% employment rate, 3% economic growth and the commitment of each Member State to a minimum of 3% of gross domestic product to invest in research and development (R&D).

In order to embed these economic objectives in the spirit of the times, this economic pillar of the strategy had to be supplemented by a social pillar aiming to improve the European welfare model and an ecological pillar stating that the economic growth pursued must be sustainable.[52]

A first intermediate report, five years after the implementation of the Lisbon strategy, was prepared under the direction of the former Dutch Prime Minister Wim Kok and showed that the strategy was failing. 'Since the deal, the European economy would have only lost competitiveness vis-à-vis the United States,' the report concludes.[53] In 2010 it was only possible to conclude that the EU strategy to get Member States to invest heavily in research and development had largely failed. The 3% standard for R&D would only be achieved by the Scandinavian countries at the end of the Lisbon process. The EU also scored particularly poorly in terms of economic growth and employment. That is why it was decided to play overtime. The Lisbon strategy was continued mutatis mutandis and renamed the Europe 2020 strategy. The employment target was raised to 75% of the population in work by 2020. Given the increasing importance of climate, the 20/20/20 objective was added (20% fewer greenhouse gas emissions than in 1990, 20% of energy from renewable energy sources and a 20% increase in energy efficiency).[54] Finally, the social pillar was provided by adding the target that fewer than 10% of Europeans should drop out of education early and at least 40% of 30–34-year-olds should complete higher education. And finally, at least 20 million fewer people should live in poverty or social exclusion.

In concrete terms, this meant that between the year 2000 and 2020, Europe's strategy was to close the gap with the United States with the aim of getting as many Europeans into work as possible and ensuring that they are as wealthy as Americans. Is that really the essence of European unification?

---

52 For a detailed analysis we refer to R. AERNOUDT, *Duurzaam ondernemen in Europese context [Sustainable Entrepreneurship in a European Context]*, Garant, 2001.

53 'Facing the Challenge', Report from the High-level Group chaired by Wim Kok, European Commission, 2005.

54 The percentages are regularly adjusted at the European Councils of Ministers, where Europe aims to be one of the most ambitious continents in terms of environmental standards. This process ultimately led to the goal of a CO_2-neutral continent by 2050.

4. CLIMATE RALLIES

European citizens found the ambition of the climate goals to be insufficient. Crowds of young people took to the streets. The movement started in Sweden and spread to most other European countries. Whether one was for or against these demonstrations, it was the voice of the citizen that resounded and determined policy. I myself attended the climate conference in Madrid from Europe, and yes, it was impressive. After the COVID-19 crisis, the movement got going again with a new climate conference in Glasgow in November 2021. The theme had become sustainable.

The new President of the Commission, the first female President, listened to it. The theme of her tenure was to be the Green Deal. The multi-year budget for 2021–2028 would largely be devoted to climate and the environment. Massive investments in energy efficiency, eco-friendly technology, eco-innovation, cleaner, cheaper and healthier modes of private and public transport, the low-carbon energy sector and energy-efficient buildings would set the coming investment agenda. The European Parliament was enthusiastic, as was the European Council, but the budget talks dragged on. In addition to those massive investment programmes, the traditional policy issues and the diminished revenues as a result of Brexit, the Member States were asked to dig a little deeper into their budgets. Denmark, the Netherlands, Sweden and Austria, disparagingly referred to as the 'frugal four', took over the role of the UK and opposed an expansion of the EU budget. The budget discussions were deadlocked. The new President of the European Council, the Belgian Charles Michel, ran from here to there to get them to sing from the same hymn-sheet. And then came the little, invisible virus that turned the whole European agenda upside down. Now there was only one priority: to avoid an economic recession and a public health catastrophe.

5. THE COVID-19 CRISIS

Like any crisis, the COVID-19 crisis made the impossible possible. Just before the crisis, there was a big fuss when Europe, on the basis of its exclusive competence in the field of competition, banned the merger between Alstom and Siemens. The Germans and the French agreed that the competition legislation had to be adjusted. By avoiding such mergers, Europe could not compete with global players. After all, in a global market it is not the market share within Europe that counts, but the global market share.

I had a sense of déjà vu. As chief of staff in Wallonia, I was involved in the merger of Arcelor, later Mittal-Arcelor. The Commission argued that the new group would have 70% of the European market and would not approve the merger until the group divested a few business units. We – I sat, temporarily, on the other side of the table – argued that the new group would represent only 3% worldwide and that the steel market is by definition a globalized market. The Commission persisted and a number of production units, such as Les Forges de Clabecq, were sold to an Italian–Swiss trading company, Duferco.[55] Yes, I also thought that competition law in Europe urgently needed to be modernized and that Europe's restricted vision on the matter was a competitive disadvantage, but the revision was out of the question at the time.

What the German–French tandem could not do, COVID-19 could. State aid was in many cases no longer considered to be anti-competitive and the Commission rapidly approved massive state aid. More than 800 state aid measures from Member States were approved in the context of the COVID-19 crisis, unseen.[56] Vaccines were jointly purchased. The Commission has even developed new support measures at lightning speed, almost doubling its budget. And what had never been possible before suddenly became possible. The Commission would raise €750 billion from the financial markets. Even Germany, which has always been reluctant to issue Eurobonds, has made a volte-face. The 'frugal four' resisted a little and demanded that a large part be done through credits and not through subsidies, but knew themselves that in times of COVID-19 they could only win their battle cosmetically.

6. MAKE EUROPE GREATER AGAIN

Let us not lose the new impetus caused by COVID-19. When necessary, Europe can make things happen. If there is one thing to learn from the crisis, it is that if we all pull together in Europe, we need not be at all inferior to America or China. Geopolitical considerations must therefore leave a mark on economic events. We should not be afraid of any kind of economic egocentrism. Let us make Europe greater again. Let us see where

---

[55] My minister, who led the negotiations at the time, Serge Kubla, later became a consultant at Duferco, which led to the end of his political career.

[56] Figures based on published Temporary Framework factsheet, August 2021, https://competition-policy.ec.europa.eu/state-aid/coronavirus/temporary-framework_en.

we can make a difference in Europe, where we are strong. And from this perspective, let us find out what more we need to do for and with Europe.

We have to look for our own unique selling proposition (USP). Europe is a values-driven society with respect for people and planet. Our diversity is not a handicap, but an asset. Diversity is the source of innovation, not uniformity. Yes, we want all Europeans to have access to health care. No, we do not want American situations where health care is for the happy few. America is not a model (except for the slogan). We should not be chasing after China either. Economic liberalism within the straitjacket of a communist one-party state model is not sustainable. And Europe is further integrating through democratic procedures, not through occupation attempts like Russia is doing with the Crimea and Donbas regions. We must impose our values on all who want to trade with Europe, take trade sanctions where needed and bury our Calimero complex.

I write values, not standards. Europe should not want to regulate everything and do everything. 'Be great in big things, small in small things.' I compare Europe to a company that has to go back to its core activities because it has diversified too much – lean and mean, a Europe focused on those areas where it can make a tangible difference for citizens.

CHAPTER 4
THE TWELVE LABOURS OF HERCULES

Based on that pragmatic approach, I have selected twelve domains, twelve labours of Hercules as illustrated on the metopes of the Temple of Zeus at Olympia. Both Hercules and Europa are part of the Greek mythology, from the cradle of European civilization, and are even interconnected. We know that Zeus disguised himself as a white bull to seduce Europa. That same Zeus used the same technique, disguising himself, this time as Amphitryon, the spouse of Alcmene, and conceiving with her a child, Hercules. The mother was considered the tallest, most beautiful woman, and wise with it. The child inherited from his natural father the combination of enormous strength and a certain leanness and was thus very powerful. By analogy, the power of Europe is based on the synergy and power of the constituent Member States and pragmatism should hence allow each of the Member States to be better off together.

The reader should see these twelve priorities as an illustration of how a pragmatic approach can work in practice. Other domains can be added and domains can be omitted, but always based on the premise that actions on the European level should make a difference and that citizens should be able to feel this in everyday life. And just as no metopes stands alone,[57] these twelve policy areas must also become holistic, rather than a menu to select from.[58]

My aim is to briefly summarize each of the labours and still – it is becoming more difficult now – avoid Eurocrat jargon. I will discuss for each labour the potential impact on European citizens and what it is all about.

---

[57] A. Blanshard, *Hercules, een Heldenleven [Hercules, a hero's life]*, Globe, 2007.

[58] I also used a similar approach in my vision for the future of Belgium, *Coronavirus: electroshock voor België [Coronavirus: electroshock for Belgium]*, Van Gompel & Svacina, 2020.

Let us not forget Jean Monnet's earlier thought that Europe is not for the Member States, but for the citizens. The twelve labours, or priorities, are:

1. Erasmus4All or the happy few?
2. Environmental and climate policy: a sense of urgency
3. Europe: a home for industry?
4. Space travel: fly me to the moon
5. Corporate policy: a mindset
6. Innovation: innovate or die
7. Internal market: the European pearl
8. The euro and monetary policy: The End of Friedman
9. Economic policy: Keynes is back
10. Work4All: between rights and benefits
11. Social and regional policy: share the benefits
12. Foreign and migration policy: towards a loyal playing field

1. ERASMUS4ALL OR THE HAPPY FEW?

Slowly die those who do not travel

Pablo Neruda[59]

The reader may wonder why the Twelve Labours of Hercules begin with a student programme. Well, the future of Europe lies with its youth. If young people do not give Europe a warm heart, there is no support for Europe. As Jacques Delors put it: how can we ever build Europe if the youth do not see it as a collective project and a vision for the future? 'The youth must take the lead in the debate on the future of Europe,' stated Ursula von der Leyen in her State of the Union address, her opening speech of the parliamentary year in 2021 and she declared 2022 to be 'the year of the youth'.

In order to create that support, we have to be pragmatic, apart from the lofty speeches. If students en masse complete part of their studies in another country, this will automatically bring an end to narrow and

[59] P. Neruda, *The Poetry of Pablo Neruda*, edited by Ilan Stavans, Farrar Straus Giroux, 2015.

dogmatic thinking. Through the Erasmus exchange, 'the Other' is no longer the unknown, but acquires a face and steps out of anonymity, referring to Levinas.[60] The 'Other' is then no longer some culture that one knows only from books, or worse from clichés, but a reality of people with whom one has studied, with whom one has cohabited, gone to bed, and has tried to make oneself intelligible in a semi-common language. The circle of friends becomes European; there are international marriages and divorces and long-life relationships.

For them, language has become a pure tool for communication. Erasmus students therefore do not deal with language as dogmatic as Europhobes. Erasmus students think less in terms of 'we' and 'them', but in terms of 'us'. Erasmus students are the building blocks of Monnet's citizens' Europe. The Erasmus programme, which is about people and not about structures, is therefore a concrete interpretation of that kind of Europe.

The programme is also economically important in a European context, as it also allows Erasmus students to work and study in a different culture and language. Multilingualism and polyculture strengthen their position in the international labour market.

But even more important is the mindset. Those who are monolingual and who never travel are always right.[61] Those who only know their own culture are culturally poor and will regard any other culture as strange, alienating. The Englishman and woman who participate in Erasmus will find that English is not the only language and will feel compelled to learn others, which will significantly improve their chances in the professional world. Belgians who participate in an Erasmus programme will regard the battle between Flemish and Walloons as old-fashioned and outdated. For them it becomes an and–and story, not an or–or story. They are Flemish (or Walloon or Brusseleir) and Belgian and European. And that, of course, applies to all countries. Erasmus changes a dogmatic attitude into a pragmatic attitude. There is no longer room for -isms (chauvinism, regionalism, nationalism, Europeanism, racism, extremism, etc.).

If such an Erasmus4All is well thought out, on the basis of reciprocity, it is indeed a fairly economic formula. The marginal cost for the educational institutions is almost nil and, if well organized, accommodation can be

---

60 E. Levinas, *Humanism of the Other*, University of Illinois Press, 2005.

61 For an in-depth analysis, see R. Aernoudt, *Wake-Up Belgians*, Roularta Business Books, 2018.

done on a reciprocal basis. It is therefore a programme at minimum cost, but with maximum economic and cultural benefits. So yes, let us make it big and make an arrangement where all university and college students have to include at least six months of Erasmus as part of their academic journey. It would solve many intercultural problems and give Europe a real identity.

Furthermore, one of the biggest losses from Brexit is the fact that the renowned English universities (Cambridge, Oxford, London) are no longer part of the Erasmus programme. The reason was that it was unacceptable to the British that European (non-British) students could study at British universities through an exchange programme without having to pay the exorbitant registration fees. Anyone who wants to study at British universities since Brexit will have to pay a great deal of money and go through complicated and expensive VISA procedures. It is disappointing that short-term financial and economic considerations now limit student exchanges with the United Kingdom to the happy few. Is that not the exact opposite of the whole process of democratization of education that we Europeans have held so dear for decades?

Interestingly, the vast majority of younger Britons voted against Brexit and now have to pay the price of a future set by the older generation. Intergenerational solidarity turned upside down.

Box 4. Erasmus for young entrepreneurs

Why should we limit the Erasmus idea to students? We should involve as many population groups as possible in European exchange programmes. There is – for the time being, still small-scale (for 10,000 entrepreneurs) – a programme for entrepreneurs. It offers young entrepreneurs the opportunity to work for up to six months with an experienced enterprise based in another EU country. The young entrepreneur, defined as someone who has been working for less than three years or has plans to start his own business, receives, in a similar principle to the Erasmus grant, a monthly sum from the European Commission that helps cover part of the expenses. So yes, there is already an Erasmus for entrepreneurs, but that should be extended as well to an Erasmus4All young entrepreneurs.

2. ENVIRONMENT AND CLIMATE: A SENSE OF URGENCY

70% of young people under the age of eighteen consider climate change as a global emergency.

Oxford University and UNDP
October 2021[62]

The fact that young people are important for the future also means that they should be able to help determine that future and, with the exception of Brexit, they do so. Youngsters have placed the climate and environmental issue high on the political agenda. Although there is something to be said about the means of communication they have used, let us be a little bit Machiavellian about this and focus on the result. Europe must become the world's first CO_2-neutral continent by 2050. The first step is a reduction of CO_2 emissions of no less than 55% by 2030, with 1990 as the reference point. Ambitious, but not unrealistic.

To achieve this objective, a package of measures, the Fit for 55 package, is being taken. To this end, six environmental objectives have been agreed: climate change mitigation, climate change adaptation, protection of water and marine resources, transition to a circular economy, pollution avoidance, and protection of biodiversity and ecosystems. An economic activity is labelled as environmentally friendly if it contributes substantially to one of these objectives without harming any of the other five.[63] This approach is called the EU Taxonomy and will determine all economic activities in the future. Those who meet the taxonomy receive the label 'green investment'.

That same taxonomy will also determine whether a bond issue can be categorized as a green bond. And many grants, such as the next-generation programme, will largely fund activities that conform to this taxonomy. Besides the programme itself, a €750 billion recovery programme is largely funded by green bonds.

By way of illustration and referring to a current debate in different European countries, let us have a look at the controversial example of nuclear energy. Nuclear energy contributes to the goal of combating global warming, because nuclear energy scores particularly well in terms of CO_2 emissions. Although the impact on the other five objectives

62 Oxford University and UNDP, 'The G20, Peoples' Climate Vote', 25 October 2021, https://www.undp.org/publications/g20-peoples-climate-vote-2021.

63 The substantial contribution and do no significant harm principles.

(the 'do no significant harm' principle) is quite complex, the technical expert group for sustainable financing concluded after a thorough analysis that nuclear energy is not more harmful to the other objectives than the alternatives. Nuclear energy can therefore, from the perspective of the European taxonomy, be regarded as green energy.[64] It was only after the crisis in Ukraine resulted in an energy crisis that countries like Belgium and Germany realized that the closure of their nuclear power plants was a political mistake. Let us focus on environmentally friendly dismantling and recycling of obsolete nuclear power stations and further investing in efficient, modern and naturally clean and CO_2-neutral nuclear power stations, and also in alternative energy sources. In this, I support French President Emmanuel Macron's decision to invest in new mini-nuclear installations as well as the decision of the UK government to build eight new nuclear reactors.

To achieve a reduction of CO_2 emissions of 55%, the reduction must of course be programmed. To this end, Europe has designed a unique instrument, the EU Emissions Trading System, which is a cap-and-trade system. Emission rights can be traded. Those who have too many can sell; those who have too few can buy.[65] As the limits are lowered annually, it becomes more expensive for those who need emission allowances. The solution is then to invest collectively to reduce emissions.

The system was first applicable to the energy, chemical and steel sectors and was expanded to other sectors as part of Fit for 55, such as transport, construction, agriculture and small industry. And just like certain stocks, there is a Market Stability Reserve to smooth out market volatility, until there is not a speck in the air.

As beautiful as this principle may seem, the problem is that Europe operates in a globalized economy and therefore the additional obligations on European companies can impede competition with foreign countries. That is why the emissions trading system is completed by a system of charges that CO_2-emitting companies must pay when they enter the European market with their products. This Carbon Border Adjustment Mechanism (C-BAM) is intended to neutralize the potential distortion of competition. However, it also applies to European companies that produce outside Europe in order to avoid carbon leakage. This is because the emission of

64 Foratom, Report of the expert group installed by article 31 of the Euratom Treaty, July 2021. Position translated into a Commission proposal and accepted by the Council and the Parliament in 2022.

65 The sale of unused allowances is one of Tesla's main profit components.

greenhouse gases in the country to which production moves increases as a result of an emission reduction in Europe. If this leak were not addressed, it would not lead to a reduction in emissions, but only to a relocation of the problem. This tax is applied to the import of emission-intensive products such as iron, steel, cement, fertilizer, aluminium and electricity.

Of course, Europe cannot aim to be more Catholic than the Pope. On the contrary, Europe's pursuit of CO_2 neutrality as a continent should lead to the US and China also having the same ambitions. Only then can we really realize what the planet needs and what young people want. In that respect, the COP-26 in Glasgow was not ambitious enough and the summit only led to an adjustment of the Paris Agreements.

3. EUROPE: A HOME FOR INDUSTRY?

Build on Europe's assets as the home of industry.

Updated Industrial Strategy, 2021[66]

Does Europe's ambition to become the world's first carbon-neutral continent imply that it can no longer be a home for industry? In other words, is the climate target compatible with a continent that values its industry? Can one be both Fit for 55 and fit4industry?

The fundamental question is indeed whether there is still room for industry in Europe. As many know, in the first decade of the twenty-first century industry had a bad reputation for often polluting. Industry would rather be lost than rich. Between the year 2000 and 2010, 40% of companies with 50 employees or more left Europe wholly or partly, mainly in search of low-wage countries. Logistical problems, excessive environmental regulations, administrative burdens, tax regulations and the predominance of the unions all pushed the industry towards exit. The result of this exodus is that the specific weight of industry is less than 20% of the gross domestic product in Europe. This average hides big differences between, for example, countries such as Belgium or France, where the weight of industry is now only about 15%, and at the other end of the spectrum countries such as Germany where industry represents 25% of the gross domestic product. The UK takes a middle position with 19%.

66 https://ec.europa.eu/info/strategy/priorities-2019–2024/europe-fit-digital-age/european-industrial-strategy_en.

The exodus came to a halt in the previous decade, partly because of the rising wage costs in China and the spectacular increases in logistics costs. A container from China to Europe has become up to twenty times more expensive in recent years, while labour costs have increased by 300% in ten years (between 2005 and 2016). The question now is whether this exodus will start again because the ambitious climate targets will also drive out the remaining industry, or whether, on the contrary, there is an opportunity for companies. The Carbon Border Adjustment Mechanism aims to avoid further offshoring, but why not go one step further and bring back the 'offshore' industry? Many industries turned their backs on Europe because of the high wage costs, as we stated earlier, but the world has changed. We have already referred to the spectacular rise in Chinese wages and logistics costs. Moreover, producing in China and serving the European market from there is not really the most ecological choice. People want to produce and consume increasingly more locally, certainly since the COVID-19 crisis. Rising costs, the environmental footprint and consumer awareness mean that the profits of offshoring are no longer compensated. Many companies would actually have an interest in returning. Based on an American study, it appeared that, if you look at the total cost of industry, 57% of the former offshore companies would have an economic interest in returning, i.e. to reshore. It would be no different for Europe, although we have no studies on the matter. Studies also show that active government policies can promote reshoring, not through subsidies but, for example, through return guidance, such as identifying suitable industrial sites or training suitable personnel.

So, let us start an active reshoring policy in Europe and set up a tailor-made industry policy 4.0 to realize this objective. For example, a company that has left Belgium, Germany or France because of wage costs could now return due to the changed circumstances. Case by case, we could examine what could enable the company to decide to reshore. If the wage difference remains a decisive factor, as is the case with mass production, for example, the return may not go to the country of origin, but to a low-wage country within Europe, such as Bulgaria or Romania, where the labour cost is three times lower than in Belgium or Germany (€14 per hour compared to €42), countries that today can compete with countries such as China or Vietnam without any problems. But let us not forget that due to far-reaching digitalization, labour costs make up an increasingly limited share of the total costs. Europe could therefore pursue an active reshoring policy, analogous to the reshoring agencies in the United States and the United Kingdom. Unfortunately, it is too afraid of incurring the accusation of protectionism, which is a geopolitical choice, not an economic one.

In addition, we must make European industry more competitive with further digitalization. The road is still long here. The resilience of the industry can increase through collaboration, alliances and ecosystems. A striking example is the alliance that the Commission has set up in the field of chips and semiconductors. The market share of these strategic products is barely 9% of global capacity. By setting up an alliance of companies from the entire value chain between different companies and countries, Europe wants to increase this to 20% by 2030. Leuven's IMEC is one of the companies spearheading that alliance. Such an alliance is necessary. Just think of car companies, such as Volvo Car Gent, a Belgian-based car factory, which was shut down for months in 2021 because the chip supply from China failed – ironic for a Chinese-owned company. This philosophy reflects the aim of making Europe the home of industry as set out in the industrial strategy updated by the Commission in May 2021. The objective is a digital, green and resilient European industry. The recovery fund of €750 billion should give a boost to this. And the climate fund of €72 billion, supplemented by emission rights, should also bring solace. All this leads to favourable future prospects for industry, something that has not escaped the attention of the Americans.

Box 5. The American invasion

Until ten years ago, the big dream of European companies was to make it happen on the other side of the Atlantic Ocean. It was mainly the search for funds to finance the rapid growth that forced them to approach US capital funds, which also meant that they developed their activity mainly transatlantically.

US funds were not interested in investing in European companies expanding their operations in Europe. US venture capital funds making investments in Europe were rather unusual. In 2011, American funds participated in 359 deals on the European continent, which meant an American investment of 'only' €2.7 billion. Academic research stated that companies were more mobile than money; in other words, an exodus of European companies to America to raise funds there started.

Apparently, the American venture capitalists have now switched sides. In the COVID-19 year 2020, they invested in 1,434 deals amounting to €51 billion, almost twenty times more than ten years previously.[67] A gigantic sum. Americans are buying up European companies en masse. From London – apparently Brexit does not bother them – the big American players are watching European companies and snapping at each new round of capital. Bessemer Venture Partners, Sequoia, Lightspeed Venture Partners, General Catalyst have all pitched their tents in London. An estimated 75% of European growth companies raising capital find that capital primarily with US funds.

What explains this sudden invasion? There is no research as yet because the invasive phenomenon is still too young. So, I venture onto thin ice by putting forward a few hypotheses. Firstly, there is the COVID-19 crisis, which has led to an awareness. Few European entrepreneurs still feel like emigrating to America with all their possessions and family or making a weekly transatlantic flight. As a result, the US funds' fishing pond is shrinking and so they now have to make the move to Europe themselves if they do not want to lose opportunities. Second, the prices of the American companies are very high, precisely because the competition between the big boys is so fierce. European companies are still usually a bargain for them. Third, many US venture capital funds are swimming in money. Dry powder, it is called in the jargon. That money must be invested because money that is not invested affects the profitability of the fund. We must not forget that profitability is the basis for the carried interest, the remuneration of the fund managers, so to speak. In addition, the fund structures are such that the money raised should actually be invested in the first five years of the fund, because after that follows the disinvestment and liquidation of the fund and, ideally, all this should take place within a time span of ten to twelve years.

The 25 largest US private equity players have an estimated $500 billion in dry powder,[68] which is more than the gross domestic product of a country like Belgium, for instance. It is therefore logical that the funds

67 European venture report, PitchBook, October 2021, https://pitchbook.com/news/reports/q3-2021-european-venture-report.

68 J. Guevarra and D. Wilson, 'Half a trillion dollars of dry powder held by 25 PE firms', *S&P Global*, 24 August 2021, https://www.spglobal.com/marketintelligence/en/news-insights/latest-news-headlines/half-a-trillion-dollars-of-dry-powder-held-by-25-pe-firms-66172037.

look for opportunities in Europe, without continuing to demand that these companies move their activities. All this means that the prices of European companies are also rising and valuations are skyrocketing, which is of course good for European business leaders and investors from the very beginning.

Desotec, for example, a manufacturer of portable waste processors, was acquired by Blackstone, one of the largest US funds, from EQT, the Wallenberg family's fund, for a multiple of 21.[69] The other European bidders could not keep up with this very high price. Klarna, the first decacorn in Europe,[70] was valued at a certain point at €45 billion or a multiple of about 60, before tumbling down. Sequoia, Silver Lake and SoftBank are among the investors. These two examples are just the tip of the iceberg that we can expect post-COVID. What this means for the European economy in the longer term is anything but clear. Will this mean we have more unicorns on the continent or is it rather the harbinger of a new exodus? In any case, developing large and mature financing industry must therefore be an absolute priority for Europe.

4. SPACE TRAVEL: FLY ME TO THE MOON

The future of space is non-space.[71]

Space travel appeals to the imagination. Billionaires compete to conquer space and turn it into a tourist attraction. But what is Europe looking for in space? I was often asked that question when I was responsible for space economics and space communication.

We could classify Europe's investments under strategic autonomy, as Europe does not want to be dependent on the United States for space, let alone on China.

---

69 The multiplier is the number by which EBITDA is multiplied to calculate the entry value.

70 A start-up company with a valuation of at least $10 billion (hence 'deca-'). In order to illustrate the relativeness of the value, in one year Klarna went from €45 billion to less than €7 billion and hence lost its deca-status.

71 Basic message of my keynote speech at the ESA conference Space4Inspiration, Bilbao, 2018.

Space, from an economic point of view, roughly encompasses three sub-aspects: telecommunications, navigation and observation. Telecommunications refers to the use of satellites that enable internet and telephone traffic. The sector is mainly private, with private companies competing in the highly lucrative telecoms market. The role of the public sector here is mainly limited to regulation and the sale of licences, though certain telecoms companies are still in public hands.

The second aspect is navigation. In order not to be dependent on the American GPS system, Europe has developed Galileo, which is more efficient than the American system. Galileo, which has been operational since 2020, is an infrastructure of 30 satellites. This satellite park can provide very accurate positioning and thus enable accurate navigation. The global annual market for navigation satellite products and services was estimated to be $244 billion in 2020. Thanks to Galileo, European companies can be at the forefront of navigation applications in various fields. Initially it was thought that the private sector would also invest, but that turned out not to be the case. After all, the return is difficult to estimate in the short term and the risks are very high. The size of the project also necessitated an approach at European level.

In politics, one does not reason in terms of return on investment, but in terms of costs and benefits. Studies show that the benefits would far exceed the investment in Galileo. Consider that all sectors of the economy can benefit from faster delivery of goods to customers, with a smaller impact on the environment and more safety for road users. Agriculture, for example, will have higher crop productivity.

The third aspect of space politics concerns earth observation. Earth observation is a child of Kyoto. Measuring is knowing. In order to achieve the environmental objectives, we must therefore be able to measure. Mapping air pollution, ocean pollution, atmospheric pollution – literally – is the core task of Copernicus, the joint initiative of the European Commission and the European Space Agency (ESA).

Copernicus was a beautiful name, but it led to much controversy. The Germans found the Polish spelling with a K unacceptable. An accounting office in Stockholm with a software package also called Copernicus and which had the same NACE code as the space observation programme (which also deals with data) caused a deadlock. I was sent to Stockholm. The amiable bookkeeper did not want to push things too far, and in so doing block Europe for an accounting package that was no longer used, so I found a financial compromise, and back in Brussels everyone found the agreed amount a very acceptable solution.

Compared to Galileo, Copernicus is technically more complicated, as the satellite park consists of completely different satellites. Each time, the ESA had to develop the satellites together with European manufacturers. However, Europe can now proudly state that it has the largest Earth observation system in the world, a luxury in times where the climate is high on the agenda.

The system is very performant. In the event of earthquakes or floods, Copernicus can generate new maps in a matter of hours, making it easier for emergency services to carry out their work. The system was used during the earthquakes in Italy in 2009 and the floods in Wallonia in 2021. We can deduce that Copernicus has saved many lives. This is invaluable.

The budgets are indeed huge, but in fact it is only one euro per day per European. With the space programmes the citizen certainly has value for public money.[72]

All in all, the applications of space are very many, in all domains. To convince economic actors and citizens, the commission services mapped 4,000 possible applications, and to demystify space, we built a travelling igloo that projected the possible applications on screens in various cities in Europe. I went from capital to capital with this itinerant caravan. At one of those events, I invited a friend to speak. After his speech, he told me: 'I will be the new President of the European Social and Economic Committee and you will be my chief of staff.' That was the end of my space career.

I am convinced that space must remain one of the spearheads in the coming decades. Europe can confidently claim that it is at the top. It is now up to the private sector to develop applications and spin-offs based on the space data that are freely available to researchers and entrepreneurs. To facilitate their task, the ESA has even set up space incubators and accelerators. The box below contains some concrete examples for inspiration.

---

72 Based on studies, we calculated that every euro invested in Copernicus leads to €4 of socio-economic benefits and in a dynamic model, in which the interactions are mapped, even up to €12. For the interested reader, this is the Phoenix econometric model. Spacetec, 'Assessing the Economic Value of Copernicus: "European Earth Observation and Copernicus Downstream Services Market Study"', December 2012, https://www.copernicus.eu/sites/default/files/2018-10/GMES_GIO_LOT3_PublishableExecutiveSummary_final.pdf. This is surely one of the reasons that UK wanted to remain in the European Space Policy after the Brexit. See for instance UK Space Agency, 'Returns and Benefits from Public Space Investments 2021', March 2022, https://assets.publishing.service.gov.uk/government/uploads/system/uploads/attachment_data/file/1069132/Returns_and_Benefits_from_Public_Space_Investments_2021.pdf.

Box 6. Non-space space applications

Health

Cardiovascular disease and cancer are the leading causes of death in developed countries. Angiex cancer therapy investigates whether cells cultured in microgravity represent a valid in vitro model to test the effects of vascular targeting agents on normal blood vessels. The results could provide a model system for the design of safer drugs.

Air purification

The air filter specially developed for space stations, Airgloss, is now also used 'on Earth'.

Transportation

ICE Cubes, a Brussels company, developed a form of transport to the International Space Station. Pharmaceutical companies, for example, can send medication in a 'cube' for testing.

5. ENTREPRENEURSHIP POLICY: A MINDSET

Entrepreneurship is an anomaly in Europe.

Paul Reynolds, GEM[73]

Earlier, in the context of the target to reduce Europe's CO_2 emissions by 55% by 2030 compared to the reference year 1990, we talked about Fit for 55 as an intermediate step towards a CO_2-neutral Europe by 2050. A large part of the necessary green investments will have to be made by companies.

Europe does not excel at entrepreneurship. For a long time, being an entrepreneur was an anomaly for those who had no other choice in life, as the Global Entrepreneurship Monitor showed. Europe is the continent of family businesses, of SMEs that often do not survive the third generation. Almost every speech on enterprise policy starts with the classic opening sentence that SMEs are the backbone of the European economy. This statement, supported by many lobby groups, led to many subsidy mechanisms to support that backbone. The result is a patchwork

[73] P. Reynolds, 'Explaining variation in nascent entrepreneurship', Academia, 2003.

of measures, some more bureaucratic than others. However, the global impact is negligible.

The problem in Europe is the entrepreneurial mindset, in other words entrepreneurship. In order to define entrepreneurship, I prefer an unconventional definition formulated by Machiavelli 500 years ago: 'Entrepreneurs are simply those who understand that there is little difference between obstacle and opportunity and who can use both to their advantage.' This is a definition that is particularly relevant in times of crisis.

Entrepreneurial policy is therefore not comparable to SME policy or to any form of economic policy. Entrepreneurship has to do with the courage to start a business, grow a business and create new economic activity, but also with more intangible things such as innovation, creativity, 'out of the box' thinking, new business models, proactive behaviour and taking risks. Europe must become much more the place where this is held in high esteem.

If we translate the above into operational terms, we could define entrepreneurship as any attempt to start a new business or expand an existing business. The mindset to start or grow can be translated into a parameter, the global entrepreneurship monitor. By correlating this parameter in year n with economic growth in year n + 1, we achieve a positive correlation of 0.52.[74] Translated into policy, this means that fostering entrepreneurship is one of the best ways to create economic growth and accelerate economic recovery.

Entrepreneurial policy thus rests on an overwhelming economic justification. But there is more: entrepreneurship policy encompasses the foundation of a democratic society, where every individual has the opportunity to pursue entrepreneurial behaviour and to set up and grow their own business. Entrepreneurship offers the individual the opportunity to develop their natural constructive and creative talents and thus offers society the opportunity for continuous progress and growth. True entrepreneurship is by definition responsible and could probably be the most effective way out of the crisis.

So, the rationale for encouraging entrepreneurship is pretty clear, but how can we change a mindset? Certainly not with subsidies. Moreover, entrepreneurship policy should not be a collection of programmes introduced on an ad hoc basis, at different times and for different purposes. This usually leads to an inefficient patchwork of measures. It should be identified as its own policy with a concept and defined areas of activity.

---

74 For an in-depth analysis and concrete policy proposals, see R. Aernoudt, *Entrepreneurship: no guts, no glory*, Intersentia, 2020.

Entrepreneurship policy should be embedded in a conceptual and holistic framework with the aim of developing an environment that enables dynamic change and supports entrepreneurship.

This approach starts with respect. Entrepreneurs deserve our respect, which means that politicians, civil servants, teachers, investors, family and friends value their entrepreneurship. In this context, success and failure are too often presented as two opposing results of entrepreneurship. However, this dichotomous approach does not correspond to economic reality. Failure is indeed part of doing business. Few entrepreneurs achieve real success without having first suffered some losses. In a society where a second chance is not part of the collective mindset, a lot of entrepreneurial potential is lost. At the other end of the spectrum, jealousy is too often a response to successful entrepreneurs, who must feel guilty for being too successful, especially when it translates into material well-being. Such a society of envy is just as damaging to entrepreneurship as the lack of understanding of failure.

To start with, a business environment that promotes start-ups is needed. Barriers to entry should be low, access to start-up finance should be easy and incubators, hackathons and accelerators must be set up efficiently. In addition, creative education, the focus on skills, flexible labour markets, and adjusted taxes and social charges are just as important. Much progress has been made in Europe in terms of focus on start-ups, but still much remains to be done, for example to facilitate the start-up of a company in another country.

The business environment must be conducive to growth. Creating a single market, avoiding red tape and removing perverse tax biases that discourage growth must be part of the holistic approach, as must the availability of skilled labour, constructive unions and economies of scale. Only together can they support the entrepreneurial ambition to grow and internationalize.

The European Union has developed a holistic approach to entrepreneurship, centred on three axes:

1. developing the entrepreneurial capacity of European citizens and organizations by promoting European learning and entrepreneurial spirit;
2. creating an environment for entrepreneurs to thrive and grow by supporting start-ups, business transfers, insolvency and second chances; and
3. establishing programmes targeting groups whose entrepreneurial potential has not yet been fully exploited, such as women and young people, through entrepreneurship learning and the earlier-discussed Erasmus for young entrepreneurs.

In conclusion, to create sustainable growth and accelerate economic recovery, incentives for entrepreneurship are indispensable. It requires a holistic approach in which the policy focus must shift from start-ups to scale-ups in the coming decades. Let us not forget that strong growers provide more than 50% of employment. Entrepreneurship policy is also a good example of subsidiarity. The exchange of best practices and the benchmarking approach should ultimately ensure that national and regional corporate policy becomes more efficient.

Box 7. Payment morality and social responsibility

The COVID-19 crisis has led to liquidity problems at many companies. In the pandemic year 2020, only two out of three invoices were paid at the agreed time; 15% of invoices remained unpaid 90 days after the agreed due date. It is estimated that 43% of invoices are paid late intentionally, as part of the financial policy. The default rate – invoices that were never paid and are therefore taken into account – amounted to 3.5% of all invoices. That is a huge percentage that affects the profitability of many companies or further increases the losses post-COVID-19.

Knowing that receivables make up an average of 25% of the total balance sheet and can amount to 40% for certain sectors, such as wholesale, one can estimate the scope of the problem. It is therefore not surprising that European studies show that late payments are one of the biggest problems for 36% of companies. In the 2021 Intrum report,[75] half of respondents indicated that late payment reduced their liquidity during the COVID-19 crisis – compared to 35% before the crisis – and a whopping 38% said it threatens their survival. One in four business failures is directly related to late payments. Needless to say, certain sectors and companies have more problems than others. The European Commission calculated that reducing the average payment terms by one day would result in a financial reduction of €158 million.

Large companies can take up their social responsibility here by paying their suppliers, often SMEs, as quickly as possible. There are European directives and transpositions into national laws about this. However, I am not talking about the law here, but about payment morality.

---

75 Intrum, 'European Payment Report 2022', https://www.intrum.be/nl/business-solutions/rapporten-en-inzichten/reports/european-payment-report-2022/.

It is in the interest of large companies that their suppliers do not have liquidity problems. So, let all large companies include in their code of conduct their policy about prepayment and short-term payment. In the Netherlands, many large companies have signed the PayMeNow charter, in which they undertake to pay invoices within 30 days. Perhaps large companies in other European countries should take a similar action. It would make business more bearable for many SMEs in these difficult times. In addition, venture capitalists, who are often required to extend the payment terms upon entering the company, can sign up to less working capital. Examples where payment terms were doubled on entry and where SMEs cannot do anything given the dominant position of the customer are commonplace. This is good for the Days Payable Outstanding (DPO) and profitability, but challenging for the suppliers.

And then look at the government. The government is a major buyer of goods and services. An estimated 18% of all purchases are government purchases. It should therefore also be the case that all local and regional transactions show a respectful payment morality. Hopefully the COVID-9 crisis can bring about a change in mentality here, as that too is the issue.

6. INNOVATION POLICY: INNOVATE OR DIE

Europe invents,
America innovates,
China imitates[76]

Europe is often perceived as the continent of times gone by. Start-ups based on innovative ideas and scale-ups are associated with the United States. Mass production is associated with China, where intellectual property rights are not taken too seriously. Often reference is made to the lack of entrepreneurship discussed above, the fragmentation of the market and the lack of financing as the causes of Europe's lagging behind. Is this perception, as formulated in the quip above, or reality?

---

76 Question submitted to European Commissioner Carlos Moedas at TEDx Brussels by me as curator.

6.1. FACTS AND FIGURES

Looking at the previous decade (2009–2019), Europe (the EU-28) has spawned 36% of global start-ups (versus 45% for the US and 17% for Asia). Consequently, and contrary to popular belief, there is no such thing as a European start-up gap, but Europe (the EU-28) has only 14% of the unicorns (versus 50% for the US and 33% for Asia). European start-ups are about 30% less likely than start-ups in the US.[77] Despite liquid financial markets, the scale-up gap (lack of venture capital available to finance scale-ups) is still very large. The search for larger amounts remains problematic. Of all successful start-ups that emerged in Europe, no less than 45% moved to the United States in the scale-up phase, a huge loss for Europe, for employment and for intellectual property. Just think of companies such as the French Criteo, the Estonian Skype or the Belgian Collibra, all companies that followed their financiers and therefore have mainly expanded their activities from America because these money-hungry start-ups in Europe could not raise the money to finance their crucial burn rate.

To illustrate, Skype was looking for €115 million. An average European fund is €65 million. If we apply the principle of sound management, a fund may invest a maximum of 10% in one investee. So, Skype would have had to convince about twenty funds to raise its money, which was almost impossible and so the company went transatlantic, where mega-funds can handle such investments. The scale-up gap should be a European priority.

6.2. COOKING COSTS MONEY

InvestEU – the European SME financing programme with a budget of €26 billion for the period 2021–2028 – provides guarantees to banks that grant loans to SMEs and invests in European venture capital funds. An additional insolvency instrument provides guarantees to banks that grant subordinated loans to companies to rebuild working capital. These programmes operate through accredited financial institutions. One of those programmes is ESCALAR, specifically aimed at closing the scale-up gap.[78]

---

[77] McKinsey, 'Europe's start-up ecosystem: Heating up, but still facing challenges', October 2020, https://www.mckinsey.com/industries/technology-media-and-telecommunications/our-insights/europes-start-up-ecosystem-heating-up-but-still-facing-challenges.

[78] ESCALAR (European Scale-Up for Risk Capital) provides for a doubling of the investment capacity of venture capital funds through the mobilization of private

With €10 billion, the European Innovation Council focuses on innovative companies with a programme to stimulate innovation. It translates this objective with programmes to support the research, validation and acceleration of technologies that can represent a European breakthrough. So, it is not about incremental innovation, but rather about disruptive innovation. The amount of aid can range from €3 million (pathfinder phase) to €18 million (acceleration phase) per company. These programmes work with project calls.[79]

In addition, a €20 billion innovation fund, mainly financed by emission rights, is in the pipeline to finance the switch to low-carbon technologies. The European Investment Bank is also setting up a loan facility for this transition, targeting the EU-10 countries.

In order to facilitate financing in the months before the IPO of companies, a pre-IPO fund is being set up. Complementary to this, the second phase of the capital market union is being launched. The aim is, among other things, to prevent fragmentation, to facilitate listing rules, to make Europeans more financially literate and to oblige banks to refer the company to other financiers in the event of a refusal of credit.

Finally, we quote DEBRA (Debt Equity Bias Reduction Allowance), which aims to tax equity financing by neutralizing the tax discrimination with debt financing, a form of European notional interest, but sustainable and significant.

All these measures should make companies fit4finance, a must after the COVID-19 crisis and the Ukraine conflict, both having severely affected the liquidities of companies.

But Europe's real added value in innovation lies not in the manna of available funds, but in the fact that to qualify for most of these funds, companies have to work together. Large companies are being asked to collaborate with smaller companies, with universities and with research institutes, across borders. Innovation is based on collaboration and diversity. It is based on combination, argued the European innovation economist Joseph Schumpeter, on the process of creative destruction. In the spirit of Schumpeter, Europe must further stimulate cooperation and

---

finance. This policy was based on my earlier research launching the concept of scale-up gap. See R. Aernoudt, 'Executive forum: the scale-up gap: and how to address it' (2017) 19(4) *Venture Capital* 361–372.

79 To illustrate: in May 2022, the European Innovation Council launched the 'Scale-Up 100' call for business support organizations, to facilitate companies with high-growth potential on their path to become European deep-tech champions.

let go of technologies and products of the past and focus on the future. Europe scores well in creativity but fails in destruction, as it keeps lame ducks alive too long. Innovation policy aimed at cooperation must remain one of the pillars of Europe. Together with the open mind through an Erasmus4All, innovation can ensure economic growth and help achieve the environmental objectives. New technologies should lead to cleaner energy, hydro-motors and so on. In this, I agree with Bill Gates, who argues that massive commitment to innovation is the best way to a CO_2-neutral world.[80]

Box 8. Deep-tech innovation

The European Innovation Council specializes in deep-tech projects. Deep tech refers to investment and innovation based on scientific progress and new discoveries. They are often projects that require collaboration across borders, are very groundbreaking and require a lot of funding. For such projects, Europe can make the difference, together with private industry. Each and every one of these projects can put Europe on the innovative map and improve the quality of life of European citizens.

Some examples:

CorWave is a French medical technology start-up developing an implantable heart pump based on groundbreaking wave membrane technology.

NIL Technology is a Danish start-up developing optical sensing and 3D imaging technologies.

Bionomous is a Swiss start-up, a spin-off of EPFL (Ecole Polytechnique Fédérale de Lausanne), with the aim of building devices to automate the visual inspection, sorting and dispensing of small biological entities. The company has developed the 'EggSorter', which is particularly suited to research in the life science industry to help find new treatments, conduct toxicology tests or better understand the biology and genetics of living organisms.

Virofight proposes a radically new approach to fighting viral infections. Rather than targeting viral proteins through small molecules, as many

80 B. Gates, *How to Avoid a Climate Disaster?*, Penguin Books, 2021.

current antivirals do, the company uses prefabricated nanoshells to capture and neutralize whole viruses. This new approach could result in a broad antiviral drug.

Neurotwin relies on non-invasive brain stimulation as an option for conditions such as epilepsy or Alzheimer's disease. Personalized hybrid brain models that unite the physics of electromagnetism with physiology – neurotwins – can play an important role in understanding and optimizing the effects of stimulation at the individual level.

7. THE INTERNAL MARKET: THE EUROPEAN PEARL

A potential welfare gain of average 840 euros per year per EU citizen.

Bertelsmann Foundation[81]

The European economy operates and innovates in a market of 450 million consumers. The *marché commun* is and remains the masterpiece of Europe. Many citizens talk about this when they talk about what is officially called the European Union.[82] Support measures and monetary expansion are interesting tools if the market temporarily fails, but the market remains the engine of the economy and it should splutter as little as possible. The internal market, in which as many obstacles to free movement as possible are removed, is therefore the pearl of the European construction and was also its first goal. The achievement took place in several phases.

In its first ten years (1958–1968), the European Community succeeded in dismantling all internal tariff barriers. Then the process of economic integration came to a halt until the Unity Act, which ended the right of veto, and this allowed a new impetus. After the tariff, the non-tariff barriers would now also be identified and phased out. Europa '92 gave a new impetus to the European project and lifted the European institutions

81 G. Mion and D. Ponattu, 'Estimating economic benefits of the Single Market for European countries and regions', Bertelsmann Stiftung (ed), 2019.

82 My blessed father always said that his son worked at the *Marché commun* in Brussels.

out of the paralysis that had characterized them after the euphoria of their founding.

7.1. THIRD-BEST SOLUTION[83]

After the completion of the first phase of the internal market, namely the abolition of tariff barriers, divisions arose within the European institutions. The right of veto, translated into an empty-seat policy, paralysed the process of European integration. Projects remained in the drawer of enthusiastic bureaucrats who gradually lost the impetus of their pioneering role and settled down into their golden cage. Unknown Commission presidents have succeeded one another and probably few readers will be able to name them. The process of European integration was deadlocked and every EEC summit was a flop.[84]

And then came Jacques Delors. The man had a vision, which he had already proven as Minister of Finance and Education in France. But he presumably realized quite quickly that he had boarded the *Titanic*. He had had no other choice. In order to set the European movement on a new course, Delors looked for various alternatives. In order of priority, he came up with the following list: the realization of a monetary union, the start of a common foreign and defence policy, and the completion of the internal market.

Again, his first choice seemed impossible. The divisions among the Member States were too great and the time was not right to give up national monetary hegemony. The European Currency Unit (ECU) was a basket of coins and annual currency adjustments were necessary to keep the European monetary system afloat. There was absolutely no question of a monetary union. The project was therefore put on hold and would only be taken out of the Eurocrats' drawers years later, following the Maastricht Treaty.

Then the second choice: a common foreign and defence policy. There, too, the national sensitivities were far too great and the water far too deep. Renunciation of defence authority had already been attempted in 1954 and apparently the time was not yet ripe. And as far as foreign policy was

---

83 Based on R. Aernoudt, *Duurzaam Ondernemen in Europese context [Sustainable Entrepreneurship in a European Context]*, Garant, 2001.

84 As a young humanities student I already dreamed of a united Europe. In order to add some real value to my childhood dreams, I decorated my student room with a large poster that read: 'EEC summit, a flop'. Psychoanalysts may see it as the harbinger of my later European vocation.

concerned, the Member States also had no intention of transferring it to the Brussels bureaucrats. Thatcher was quite sharp and was not alone in her plea.

Then the third choice: the realization of the internal market. The project had been in the drawers of Brussels bureaucrats since the 1960s. It was Delors' contribution to blow the dust off the files and it was a brilliant marketing stunt to put a date on the realization. Europa '92, the queen piece, was born.

7.2. THE UNITY ACT

The objective of a single internal market was already enshrined in the Treaty of Rome. At that time, however, they had not progressed beyond the creation of what is called a customs union. All tariffs hindering the movement of goods between Member States had been abolished. In addition, a common external rate was agreed for all products. Precisely because of this, the European Community distinguished itself from that other club founded at the time by the United Kingdom, the European Free Trade Area.

But in order to really speak of a single market, all barriers to trade must also be removed. Only then can one speak of the so-called four freedoms: free movement of persons, goods, services and capital. We collectively refer to the various obstacles as all obstacles that are not tariffs, or in other words the non-tariff obstacles. These are obstacles that can be classified into material, technical and fiscal obstacles. The services of the European Commission identified 282 of these obstacles and so an equal number of decisions had to be taken. It is not surprising that the plan remained in the drawer of the Eurocrats for about twenty years. In fact, three elements were missing to be able to implement the plan: first of all, the political will; secondly, the necessary decision-making procedure; and finally, the proof of the economic importance of the project.

If Delors, with his charisma and support from his homeland, succeeded in convincing the political leaders of the need to revive the European project, this could of course only be realized through adequate decision procedures. Making nearly 300 decisions when everyone at the table had a veto right was an impossible task. First, the Treaty of Rome had to be amended. The first major amendment to the Treaty of Rome was the Unity Act, which entered into force on 1 July 1987. This replaced the unanimity rule with the qualified majority rule in many areas. After reaching an agreement on the target, the 282 individual measures could be taken with a qualified majority. This translated the political will into a legal framework to make it happen.

Then the economic importance still had to be demonstrated. Was the single market economically justifiable? To answer this question, a working group was set up under the leadership of the Italian economist Cecchini. The combined effect of the elimination of customs formalities, the opening of public markets, the liberalization of financial services and capital flows, and increased competition would profoundly affect the economic environment in Europe. This would translate into lower inflation, more employment and more economic growth. The impact on economic growth was estimated at 3.2–5.7% of gross domestic product, with an increase in employment of 1.3–2.3 million jobs and all this with a fall in inflation by 4.5–7.7%. Euro-sclerosis gave way to Euro-phoria. And in the slipstream of this Euro-phoria, I said goodbye to my banking career and started my career as a Eurocrat.

7.3. SINGLE MARKET: STILL UNDER CONSTRUCTION

This political, legal and economic concept, together with the ingenious move to put a target date on it, made the single market a reality by the end of 1992. Almost 90% of all decisions have been transposed into national law: more passenger rights, assistance for service providers across borders, cheaper telephone calls and better protection of savings are just some of the many benefits of the internal market. But is it all roses and moonshine?

A quarter of a century later, the single market is still not a reality. It must be said that most of the obstacles have been removed and customs formalities have largely been abolished, but important dossiers necessary to ensure the proper functioning of the market have been under construction for years. For example, the Nice Summit at the end of 2000 paved the way for the creation of the European company, but it still does not exist. Passport controls are still not completely abolished, especially in the non-Schengen countries. They are often even reintroduced in the fight against terrorism or used to contain a pandemic. And starting a business in another country remains a feat.

The project gave a new impetus to European thinking and had undeniably positive effects on the economy. A report by the Bertelsmann Foundation calculated that the welfare gains of EU citizens per capita amounts to an average of €840 per year, albeit with strong differences between the different countries.[85] However, the non-completion of the internal market means that a great economic potential remains untapped. For example, the European Parliament's study bureau calculated that the completion of the internal market could yield €2,200 billion in economic benefits, which corresponds to 14% of the European gross domestic product.[86]

Some of the proposals were launched by the Juncker Commission as part of the Deeper and Fairer Single Market programme. A lot of progress has been made in areas such as the European digital market, the integrated energy market or the banking union, but the work is not yet finished. So, it remains an absolute priority. A Delors-bis project, with a list of necessary measures and a target date, would again be useful. It is high time to finish the gigantic construction site, comparable to the Sagrada Familia in Barcelona.

7.4. THE CONNECTED FOUR FREEDOMS

The Commission invariably observes that the internal market is not a menu from which to choose. Most countries are enthusiastic about the free movement of goods, services and capital, but the free movement of persons is a sensitive issue. Countries belonging to the European Economic Area (the EU and Liechtenstein, Norway and Iceland) must therefore respect the four freedoms. Those who want to enjoy the advantages of the internal market must also take the disadvantages into account, say the Eurocrats. David Cameron, the former British Prime Minister, requested to adjust the child benefits of Eastern European workers in his country to be in line with longevity in their home country. That was refused by the European Commission and especially considered illegal by the European Court of Justice. After all, the Court's task is to ensure compliance with European legislation and the Court left no room for compromise manoeuvres. The British felt crippled in their sovereignty and, according to insiders, that was the last straw that provoked the launch of the Brexit referendum.

An analogous situation can be found in Switzerland, which is not part of the European Economic Area. Advanced discussions in 2021 were

---

85 Bertelsmann Stiftung, 'Estimating economic benefits of the Single Market for European countries and regions', 2019.

86 *Mapping the cost of non-Europe*, European Parliamentary Research Service, 2019. The document analyzes 24 areas for which the completion of the internal market is necessary and calculates the economic impact in each case.

unilaterally suspended by Bern because unimpeded passenger traffic was a bridge too far. Even the trade unions were opposed because they feared that an uncontrolled influx of migrants would jeopardize high wages and the generous social security system.

Both examples show that the economic benefits of the single market through the free movement of services, goods and capital are often not convincing enough to accept the principle of free movement of persons. The preservation of sovereignty in this matter often appears to outweigh the acceptance of an open border policy, in which the European Court can act as arbitrator. It led to Brexit and is clouding relations between Europe and Switzerland and complicating the border traffic of goods and services.

However, the completion of the internal market is essential if Europe is to reap the full economic and social benefits of the European integration process that began in the middle of the last century.

Box 9. The single market and the United Kingdom

For those who still have doubts about the internal market, it is interesting to take a look at the position of the United Kingdom. It was the outspoken anti-European Margaret Thatcher who negotiated the internal market in 1987, the year I joined the European Commission. It was her greatest achievement in free trade, and in the interest of Britain and Europe, and it turned out to be a success.

Boris Johnson, the former UK Prime Minister, saw leaving that single market as the inevitable price to pay to leave the EU. 'No Brexit without the end of the single market,' he proclaimed. Europe experts consider this view the second big Brexit lie, alongside the previously discussed savings of £350 million a week.[87]

Another lie for which the British taxpayer has to pay. The UK government's customs department[88] has calculated that an additional 215 million documents are required each year to handle export and import formalities, resulting in an annual bureaucratic cost of £7.5 billion. After all, although no import duties will be imposed – at least in the

87 S. Jenkins, 'Boris Johnson's biggest lie about Europe is finally coming home to roost', *The Guardian*, 6 September 2021, https://www.theguardian.com/commentisfree/2021/sep/06/boris-johnsons-biggest-lie-europe-coming-home-single-market.

88 His Majesty's Revenue and Customs (HRMC) department is a non-ministerial part of the UK government responsible for customs services and customs taxation.

short term – health checks and certificates of origin are now necessary. Thatcher is probably turning in her grave.

The British would have been better off deciding to leave the European Union but to remain in the internal market, as for example Norway does. Demagoguery has caused a blindness to all economic realities. The infamous immigration stops have also led to a shortage of workers, as a result of which the economy almost came to a standstill at the end of 2021 and the petrol stations were empty.

8. THE EURO AND MONETARY POLICY: THE END OF FRIEDMAN

No one falls in love with the single currency.

Jacques Delors[89]

Where the Erasmus programme gives concrete shape to Europe in spirit, the climate ambition takes care of the planet, and industry, businesses, innovation and the internal market are the basis for prosperity, the euro gives concrete shape to our purchasing power: a single market, a single currency, is the big European aspiration.

The euro acts as a powerful signifier[90] and has become the world's most powerful currency after the dollar and the yuan, accounting for about 25% of all transactions. Whenever we make a cash, cashless or digital payment, we actually show our eurozone club membership card. The euro is an acquired right, especially for Generation Z. A Deutsche Mark, a Belgian franc or a Greek drachma, to name but a few, are terms, coins or notes that, for them, evoke a relic from a distant past.

8.1. THIRD TIME'S THE CHARM

The introduction of the single currency, like the realization of the internal market, did not go smoothly. As early as 1970, the Werner Plan, named

---

89 This sentence, attributed to Jacques Delors, graces many corridors of the European Commission. The official version is that no one falls in love with the single market.

90 This is in reference to Anglo-Saxon philosophy of language.

after the then Luxembourg Prime Minister, aimed at achieving European monetary union by 1980. The global monetary crisis, which manifested itself in, among other things, President Nixon's abolition of convertibility from the dollar to gold in 1971 was one of the reasons why the Werner Plan was never realized.

Ten years later, at the initiative of West Germany and France, a second attempt was made to set up the European monetary system. The currencies of the European Union concluded an agreement that their mutual movements would be limited to a certain percentage, the European Exchange Rate Mechanism. The system provided a certain currency stability. The central theoretical currency that served as the reference currency was the ECU. The ECU is a theoretical basket of European coins whose value was thus a derived value.

As a student at the College of Europe, I wrote my thesis about the different scenarios to arrive at a single currency. From the 'big bang' scenario (the national notes and coins will one day be replaced by the new currency), to the parallel scenario (the national notes and coins will remain in circulation for a while in parallel with the new currency until the latter's introduction as a means of payment), to the scenario where the ECU, the then unit of account, would become the status of full currency into the Gresham scenario in which the market would eventually liquidate the national currencies. This last scenario referred to Gresham's law that bad coins remain in circulation because people hoard the good coins and spend the bad ones.

The 'big bang' scenario seemed unfeasible in practice. The upgrade of the ECU could never succeed because the ECU was a basket of different coins composed of the underlying coins. So that would be a vicious circle. The Gresham scenario also failed because certain currencies would be perceived as better than the new currency (such as the Deutsche Mark) and others worse (such as the constantly devaluing Italian lira, or the Belgian franc, currency of a country full of debt). Of the four scenarios, only one turned out to be possible. That was also the summary of my thesis, which now comes across as medieval to many readers, including myself, and of course contributed nothing to the final solution.

Fifteen years after the second attempt, the monetary union plan was revived, made possible in part by the Unity Act discussed above. The European Monetary Institute was established in 1994, renamed the European Central Bank (ECB) in 1998, and exchange rates were locked in on 1 January 1999. Academic analysis showed that the ECU could not get the job done. The new currency could no longer be a basket, but had to become a full-fledged currency: the euro was born. And the elimination of the national currencies could not be realized by the market forces in view of Gresham's law, but only by a law establishing the parallel period. The disappearance of the national currencies was only a material and psychological issue, which was also clearly felt in the purse from 2002. It would take three years. In concrete terms, the euro was officially introduced as a means of payment on 4 January 1999, and euro coins and notes were introduced to replace the previous national coins and notes. A considerable feat.

8.2. EUROZONE VS EUROPEAN UNION

The countries that chose to use the euro also had to coordinate their policies more closely. Controlling inflation, limited budget deficits, a reasonable level of public debt and normal interest rates were the conditions for entry. They were called the convergence criteria. A country such as Belgium that was struggling with too much debt could only join with a large-scale savings plan. The eurozone was born. Twelve of the fifteen Member States wanted to participate in the project. Of these twelve, only Greece had to put aside its ambitions for a while. It was only able to join the club in 2001. The reason was that it still had to meet certain economic criteria before it could join. Yes, we already knew that back then.

So, initially there were eleven, quickly growing to nineteen. Indeed, unlike the European Union, no member has left the club to date. On the contrary, there were always more. A number of European Union countries do not (yet) belong to the eurozone, because they have not yet reached the required economic parameters. However, a progress report is drawn up every year. So, it is only a matter of time before these countries – Hungary, Poland, the Czech Republic, Bulgaria and Romania – can join the eurozone, following the example of Croatia that has joined in 2023 as the twentieth member. All these countries must adopt the euro as soon as they meet the economic criteria.

Two countries, the United Kingdom and Denmark in particular, wanted to remain in the European Union, but did not want to relinquish their monetary autonomy and negotiated an opt-out, i.e. the right not to join. For the United Kingdom, as a side effect of Brexit, the problem has been resolved. Only the Danes, who stuck to the Danish krone through a referendum, have no accession prospects. However, this is a rather symbolic battle. Through the European Exchange Rate Mechanism, which was a system to stabilize European exchange rates in preparation for the

European Economic and Monetary Union and the introduction of the euro, the exchange rate of the Danish krone is tied to the euro. It is worth noting that anyone who has already been to Copenhagen or Aarhus has never encountered any problems paying with euros. Additionally, one may wonder whether a referendum is the right technique for the introduction of a new currency. Would the euro have been born if the participating countries had consulted their populations directly?

By way of illustration, we refer to Sweden, which did not have an opt-out and, when it joined the European Union in 1994, committed itself, like every new member, to also adopt the euro. However, in a referendum in 2003, 56% of Swedes opposed the introduction of the euro, despite the fact that the same Swedes had voted for membership of the European Union by 52% two years earlier. As a result, Sweden's entry into the eurozone was postponed, even though, unlike the six other countries mentioned above, it fulfils all the convergence criteria.[91]

In addition, there are countries outside the eurozone that use the euro as their official currency. Indeed, the euro is not only used in the eurozone countries, but is also legal tender in Monaco, San Marino, Vatican City and Andorra (which have their own euro coins). In addition, the euro is officially used in Montenegro and Kosovo, which opted for the euro as their official currency upon their independence from the former Yugoslavia. In practice, this means that the euro is the only currency used in those countries, but that it is not legal tender there according to the ECB.

8.3. THE EUROPEAN CENTRAL BANK

That brings us to the Central Bank. To keep the euro on the right track, you obviously need a Central Bank. The 'surrender' of the national currency was a big concession for Germany, which already had a very strong economy and very strong currency. It was therefore logical that the Central Bank would come to Germany, more specifically to Frankfurt.

After all, with the creation of the European Community, barely a decade after the Second World War, it was still a delicate prospect to establish a

[91] These criteria are the so-called Maastricht criteria and relate to the budget deficit (maximum 3% on an annual basis), public debt (maximum 60% of GDP), inflation (maximum 1.5% above the EU average), long-term interest rate (maximum 2% above EU average) and the exchange rate (without tensions in the last two years before joining the eurozone). The Commission produces an annual report for each non-eurozone EU country.

European institution in Germany. The European Community institutions thus started with Strasbourg, a symbolic city in Alsace that belonged alternately to France and Germany, then Brussels and Luxembourg, two mini-states squeezed between France and Germany. When the European Central Bank was established, the time had come to assign that institution to Germany. The United Kingdom, with London as its financial centre, was ineligible because it had never joined the eurozone.

The European Central Bank would thus become the counterpart of the US Federal Reserve (the Fed) and would claim the euro's place in the world next to the dollar. The ECB, founded in 1999, has to give concrete shape to European monetary policy. It has done so successfully: about one-quarter of all transactions at world level are now denominated in euros. Not bad for a currency that did not exist twenty years ago.

Both the ECB and the Fed are politically independent, yet there are differences between the US and the European approach. The Fed's job is to monitor inflation and stimulate the economy. The sole task of the ECB is to achieve the inflation target. In short, we could say that the Fed is part of economic and monetary policy, while the ECB only has monetary objectives.

This did not prevent the ECB from supporting the economy with large resources. By injecting money into the financial markets, it gave the banks breathing space so they could stimulate the economy. The interest rate was kept very low, even negative. The statements by Mario Draghi and Christine Lagarde, the governors, that they would do everything to support the economy had a positive impact on the financial and economic markets. The sums that the so-called bazooka pumped into the economy were huge. To curb the effects of the COVID-19 crisis, the ECB launched a €1,350 billion purchase programme, or about three times the gross domestic product of a country like Belgium.

The critical reader might wonder whether this is in line with the ECB's goal and will not lead to inflation. The financial crisis (2008), the COVID-19 crisis (2020) and the Ukraine conflict (2022) have caused an ailing economy. As a result, inflation has remained historically low. In concrete terms, the ECB's target to keep inflation under control means 'less than but close to 2%', a target of 1.8–1.9%, a target that it has failed to achieve for a long time. The impact of the bazooka on the economy, although partially offset by banks holding high deposits with the ECB, is real, but it is also fuelling inflation. Killing two birds with one stone, one could say, as long as inflation does not, of course, derail due to the gigantic monetary expansion, which was the case from the end of 2021, when it reached two-digit levels.

8.4. FUTURE PERSPECTIVES

Initially, no one – including many economists – ever thought that the single currency would be a success and become sustainable. Twenty years later, the euro has survived financial crises and even a euro-Grexit has been avoided.

Nobody fell in love with the euro, as Jacques Delors put it, but the euro did give Europe concrete shape. It would be easier if all the countries of the European Union joined the eurozone. After all, the currency is the expression of the economic situation of the country. The 2008 financial crisis painfully demonstrated that economic and monetary policy must go hand in hand.

So why not start bilateral negotiations with all non-eurozone EU countries to allow them to join the eurozone as soon as possible? A concrete action plan can be established with the five countries that do not yet meet the convergence criteria, as was done with Belgium at the time. A one-to-one overlap of the European Union with the eurozone would simplify governance and lead to greater coherence between economic and monetary policy. If Denmark is the only opt-out outsider, it can be bilaterally agreed with that country that it would support monetary policy. Incidentally, Denmark is a healthy, sustainable economy and its non-membership is far from problematic. Similarly, Sweden can either hold a new referendum or, like Denmark, peg its currency to the euro. Incidentally, almost all political parties in Sweden are in favour of joining the eurozone. Europe and the euro would only become stronger if almost all EU countries also were to become eurozone countries.

And as for the ECB, why should Europe be holier than the United States? Including an economic target in the ECB's statutes, in addition to the inflation target, would give it even more leeway.

Box 10. Euro cents and inflation

Since the introduction of the euro, the currency has lost 35% of its value. In other words, the contents of a shopping cart now cost 35% more than twenty years ago. 'The Euro's fault!' Eurosceptics shout. However, all studies show that there is no causal link whatsoever. But perception is often more persistent than reality. When the Commission wanted to remove the one- and two-euro cent coins from circulation at the beginning of 2022 – which had already happened already in six EU countries – it was again suggested that this would encourage inflation. Nothing could be further from the truth, because the rounding happens both upwards and downwards. Several studies have also confirmed this. But again, the power of demagoguery was stronger than the power of science.

9. ECONOMIC POLICY: KEYNES IS BACK

You cannot cut yourself out of a slump,
you've got to grow yourself out of a slump.

John Maynard Keynes[92]

In times of crisis, the government must act counter-intuitively. The monetary bazooka can only be effective if it is introduced and complemented by the real economy. Every reader has heard of General Marshall's gigantic recovery policy, just after the Second World War. In this case, the war had paralysed the economy, with the exception of the war economy. A powerful revival led to the golden sixties and the impact would last for a long time.

In fact, COVID-19 had the same impact on the economy. The economy has never been hit so hard. And in addition to a further bazooka, plus national and regional measures, Europe also had to be involved. Solidarity, a basic value of Europe, had to take concrete shape in times of crisis.

It was not easy. After four days and nights of negotiating with the 'frugal four' (the Netherlands, Austria, Sweden and Denmark, joined for the occasion by Finland) on the brakes, one of the most difficult, and in any case longest, European councils was successfully concluded with a special recovery fund and an opportunity for new own resources financing.[93] Would it have been possible if the UK had still been a member?

The special recovery fund is a good example of counter-intuitive policy. It provides for an amount of €750 billion or 4% of the European gross domestic product.[94] By comparison, the Marshall Plan was 'only' 1.5% of

---

92 R. Skidelsky, 'Keynes v Hayek: Two economic giants go head to head', *BBC News*, 3 August 2011, http://www.bbc.co.uk/news/business-14366054.

93 European summit, 18–21 July 2020.

94 See my plea for countercyclical policy in *Coronavirus: Electroshock voor België [Coronavirus:, Electroshock for Belgium]*, Van Gompel & Svacina, 2020.

gross domestic product. This support should be used for investments that are green, digital or increase the resilience of the economy. A huge amount has been financed by the issuance of mainly green bonds and made available largely through grants and partly through loans. The amounts raised are distributed to the most affected Member States to finance strategic investments in the form of grants and credits.

It was also an example of solidarity for three reasons. Firstly, the funds went to those countries most affected by the COVID-19 crisis, such as Spain and Italy. Secondly, the funds were collected through the European citizen and not through an additional endowment. Thirdly and more importantly, the financing was done through the issuance of a loan, mainly through green bonds, with all Member States jointly responsible for its repayment.

The European ban on taking on debt was thus broken and that was unique in European history. COVID-19 bonds was too sensitive as a term. Jacques Delors, the former charismatic president of the European Commission, had already tried to issue a bond to finance 'the highways of telecommunications', as he called it, but without success. He was then vetoed by the United Kingdom. After all, the European Commission works on the basis of an annual budget that must not show any deficits, and the Council rejected the taking on of credits.[95] Now the British were no longer there.

But those who incur debts must also repay them. The expiry date is 2058, so there is still time, but we also had to look for ways to generate revenue for Europe. Income for a government is commonly referred to as taxes. Since the world is so concerned with the environment – the climate demonstrations could only be stopped by COVID-19 – the solution was available. The Commission was instructed by the Council to introduce a tax on non-recycled plastics and a carbon tax on imports of 'polluting' steel. In addition, and in view of the – mainly American – digital giants who skip through life almost tax-free, a European digital tax and a minimum tax for multinationals also had to be considered. In October 2021, a worldwide historic agreement was reached through the Organization for Economic Cooperation and Development that fixed this minimum tax at 15%. It was endorsed by world leaders at the G20 summit that same month.[96]

---

95 Council of Brussels, June 1994.

96 The OECD agreement was signed by 130 countries on 11 October 2021 and foresees the introduction of a minimum tax of 15% by 2023. The G20 summit in Rome on 30 October 2021 endorsed the agreement. For certain European countries, such as Ireland, Estonia and Hungary, this implies a tax increase, and these countries have been thwarting this for a long time. Switzerland has already announced that 2023 will not be feasible. The OECD estimated the additional income at €130 billion.

With the Eurobond financing, a huge European hurdle was cleared. The breach was opened for a European lending capacity. That capacity is, of course, great and almost unlimited. It enables less creditworthy Member States to rely on European creditworthiness and consequently to obtain better conditions. It is a precedent with clear added value at European level.

The only problem with such an approach is the free rider problem. This means that certain Member States can surf on the creditworthiness of others and are therefore not inclined to take the much-needed structural measures. This is also called a bonus for bad management. This free rider problem was mitigated, at least in part, by the emergency brake that was introduced at the request of the Netherlands: Europe can stop aid if the beneficiary Member State does not take the necessary structural measures.

In addition, the breach was opened for own taxation, which incidentally corresponds to the policy priorities regarding the environment and digitalization. This double hurdle paves the way for a truly counter-intuitive policy. If the European Union continues down this path, with loan financing and new own resources, it will be able to respond appropriately to economic and monetary crises and even anticipate them. The Foresight Task Force, set up by the von der Leyen Commission, to which I also belong, can even anticipate this. If we can combine those opportunities with good governance, at European, national and regional level, then Europe's future looks bright.

Finally, and more generally, I think it is a good thing that the government that spends is also the one that collects the financing of those expenses, i.e. taxes. This way, every taxpayer can know whether he or she is getting enough value for the tax money paid. This also increases the democratic content of each policy level. In addition, one must avoid budget deficits swinging out of control and governments having a green light to build up debt for generations to come. Keynes himself argued that deficit spending should be a short-term policy and not a structural long-term policy. Let us not forget that.

10. WORK4ALL: BETWEEN RIGHTS AND BENEFITS

The government's job is to ensure that everyone has a job.

Mahatma Gandhi

European employment policy is a very sensitive topic because it is ideologically charged. It is therefore always dancing on the tightrope of subsidiarity. The general basic idea is that more people have to work in

Europe than has been the case until now. Enjoying rights and benefits without obligations should be avoided – in other words, no unconditional benefits. Due to the aging population, this is the only way to make the European social model sustainable. Employment is also the best tool in the fight against poverty, although not always the solution; consider, for example, the working poor. In any case, the basic philosophy of European employment policy is that people should work. Employability is the keyword of the European employment strategy. The European employment strategy is built around four main themes, namely employability, entrepreneurship, adaptability and equal opportunities. Member States have committed themselves to pursue this employment strategy through the implementation of the annual guidelines. The follow-up is done through a policy coordination process that was laid down in the Treaty of Amsterdam. In concrete terms, it is translated into the European semester report, which, as the name suggests, is drawn up every six months.

The objective is to achieve a participation rate of 78% of the working population (people between 20 and 64 years old) by 2030. The number of people at risk of social exclusion should fall by 15 million by then. Realizing these goals should be an absolute priority for our Europe based on socio-economic values.

Social policy remains Europe's Achilles' heel. A thorough social policy should therefore be a priority in the coming years. As a basic principle of Europe, solidarity must be linked to responsibility. It is evident that profiteers and those who are not willing to work undermine the affordability of our social system.

European coordination covers various areas of economic and social policy: structural reforms, with an emphasis on growth and employment, social and labour market policies, budgetary policies and, finally, the prevention of excessive macroeconomic imbalances. The semester reports, which are based, among other things, on social scoreboards, also provide each Member State with recommendations.

The Council can always decide to include other themes in the semester reports. On 17 November 2017, the European Parliament, the Council and the European Commission proclaimed the European Pillar of Social Rights. It contains twenty core principles for a strong social Europe in the areas of equal opportunities, labour market access, fair working conditions, social protection and inclusion. The pillar is included in the European Semester. In 2020, as part of the Green Deal, the UN Sustainable Development Goals were also included in the European Semester. Through these semester reports, Europe respects the competence of the Member

States that are responsible, for example, for employment policy, but it remains in accordance with the principle of subsidiarity.

The principle of subsidiarity, as expressed in the papal encyclicals, prescribes that 'when choosing to make a choice, preference is given to that circle of life where the activity of those involved and the chance of democratic control is greatest'.[97] Applying the principle of subsidiarity to employment means that the approach should not be European, not even national or regional, but rather local, based on a 'close to the people' approach. Unemployment is now a problem that transcends the locality and is characteristic of almost the entire European continent. Subsidiarity means that the approach should be drawn up at the highest possible level and that the implementation should take place locally. The approach to employment corresponds exactly to this: we can indeed summarize employment policy with the adage 'think global, act local'. Guidelines are established at Community level, but implementation is at a lower level.

By way of illustration, the reader will find in the box below the recommendations for the United Kingdom for 2020, the last year before the implementation of Brexit. At the same time, the box illustrates the Eurocrat jargon that I have previously criticized. Anyone who hands this text over to his or her driver would have to send it back to the administration after reading it for complete revision. However, such recommendations are also of interest to citizens.[98]

Box 11. Semester report: specific recommendations for the United Kingdom

The Council hereby recommends that the United Kingdom take action in 2020 and 2021 to:

1. In line with the general escape clause, take all necessary measures to effectively address the pandemic, sustain the economy and support the ensuing recovery. When economic conditions allow, pursue fiscal policies aimed at achieving prudent medium-term fiscal positions and ensuring debt sustainability, whilst enhancing investment. Strengthen the resilience of the health system.

---

97 H. Brugmans, 'Europa: ideaal van gerechtigheid' ['Europe: ideal of justice'], in *Europa voorbij het nulpunt, [Europe beyond zero]*, Scriptoria, 1975, p. 224.

98 Recommendation for a council recommendation on the 2020 National Reform Programme of the United Kingdom and delivering a Council opinion on the 2020 Convergence Programme of the United Kingdom, COM/2020/528 final.

2. Ensure the adequacy and coverage of the social protection system to provide support for all and in particular those most affected by the crisis.
3. Foster innovation and support human capital development. Front-load mature public investment projects and promote private investment to foster the economic recovery. Focus investment on the green and digital transition, in particular on housing, clean and efficient production and use of energy, sustainable transport infrastructures and high speed broadband networks.

11. SOCIAL AND REGIONAL POLICY: SHARE THE BENEFITS

'European integration'
not only brings winners
but also losers.

Ferdi De Ville[99]

The single market ensures greater mobility of goods and services, but production factors such as capital and labour are also becoming more mobile. Economists such as the Swedish Nobel laureate in economics Gunnar Myrdal[100] have shown that this increased mobility will lead both capital and labour to seek out the more productive regions. This means that there will be a migration of highly skilled workers from the poorer to the richer regions. Moreover, in search of a higher return on their investment, capital will flow to the wealthier regions. The single market will thus exacerbate disparities between regions. In other words, richer regions get even richer; poorer regions get even poorer.

In addition to these regional disparities, social problems will also be exacerbated. Freedom of movement for individuals may be of interest to students and senior management, but how do low-skilled workers or the physically disabled benefit from the single market, other than the fact that travel may become a little easier?

---

99 F. De Ville, *Winnaars en Verliezers [Winners and losers]*, Pelckmans, 2018.

100 G. Myrdal, 'The Equality Issue in World Development' (1989) 79(6) *The American Economic Review* 8–17.

In summary, the European welfare state is more resilient in some countries than in others and for some groups than others, so there are winners but also losers.[101]

In order to somewhat mitigate the negative impact on certain social groups and regions, it was decided to release substantial budgets for social and regional politics.

These budgets must therefore compensate for the negative effects of the internal market on certain regions and certain groups. But is it worth closing these gaps? Are public interventions needed here and would it not be better to let the market do things right, claim the ultra-liberals. Besides, after all these years of intervention, we cannot unequivocally demonstrate that the differences have decreased significantly, argue the critics of government intervention. In support of this, reference is often made to southern Italy, which, after 25 years of intervention, has still not closed the gap with northern Italy. Let market forces determine where it is good to invest, study and live, many proclaim, after American guru Michael Porter. Moreover, it is stated in the same breath that a large part of the funds that are pumped into these poorer regions do not reach those who have the most need. Fraud and corruption are rampant and the large sums associated with regional policy certainly do not escape this logic.

Economists refer to the spread effect, which means that with strong growth, rich regions run out of space, there is a shortage of industrial sites, problems with traffic mobility, it becomes increasingly difficult to find suitable offices, and so on. For all these reasons, part of the growth in the richer regions will be channelled to the poorer regions, which in this way also benefit from the growth. But studies show that the polarization effects, i.e. that capital and labour will move to the richer regions because there is more to gather there, are stronger. This makes it easier for rich regions to have well-trained personnel and sufficient capital, while the poorer regions continue to grow poorer.

So, the movers are the winners, the stayers the losers. The central regions are the winners, the peripheral regions the losers. This market failure must therefore be corrected. After all, how can the losers be lastingly convinced of the welfare effects of the internal market that are not intended for them. Social and regional policy is therefore not only necessary from a human perspective, but essential as a correlate of the internal market.

But there are still reasons why regional and social policies are needed. Where the gap between regions is large, there is also a source of conflict.

---

101 F. De Ville, *Winnaars en Verliezers [Winners and Losers]*, Pelckmans, 2018.

Poverty, and especially unequally distributed poverty, can lead to political tensions and violence and thus threaten political stability. Poverty reduction is therefore important both from a human perspective and with a view to a sustainable, safe society.

Incidentally, despite increased mobility, the mobility of production factors is never perfect. Regional policy is therefore the only way to avoid underemployment. And finally, sustainable economic growth is only possible if it is evenly distributed across the various regions.

The intensification of regional politics was thus not as noble as it might seem at first glance, but rather as a compensation for the wave of liberalization that has ravaged Europe. Many countries also regard this as a kind of indirect repayment of the contribution to the European Union and therefore want to join the regional subsidies.

But this is exactly where the shoe pinches. After all, the question must be asked whether regional policy should not be reserved only for those countries that really need it. Why should rich countries such as Belgium, France or the Netherlands receive regional aid? Sub-regions such as Hainaut, Limburg, Nord Pas de Calais or Groningen, to name just a few, should not be subsidized by Europe. It is up to the Member States to decide whether this is necessary. Europe should only focus on poorer countries so that they can keep up. Countries such as Romania and Bulgaria should be the target of a regional policy in a European context. And that this must be done as efficiently as possible and in such a way that corruption and fraud must be avoided – that is a priority.

12. FOREIGN POLICY: TOWARDS A LOYAL PLAYING FIELD

Domestic policy can only defeat us,
foreign policy can kill us.

John F. Kennedy[102]

Foreign policy concerns both geopolitical and economic aspects. I have never been a diplomat. Yes, I question Europe's attitude to Russia's illegal annexation of Crimea and Sevastopol and Europe's lack of response to the flagrant violation of women's rights in Afghanistan but applaud Europe's unanimity in condemning Russia for the Ukraine invasion. And no, I am

102 *The Imperial Presidency*, 1973.

not proud of a President of the European Council who falls into Erdogan's trap in front of the whole world and publicly embarrasses the President of the European Commission. But here I speak more as a citizen than as a Eurocrat. Since it is my intention with this book to give the reader a view behind the scenes, and as I have never been involved in diplomatic relations, I limit myself to the economic aspects of foreign cooperation.

The common commercial policy is in fact the logical counterpart of the internal market. After all, unlike the free trade zone, the European Union has a common external border. That is the essence of the Union. It is therefore not surprising that this common commercial policy was already enshrined in the Treaty of Rome. It includes negotiations on tariff changes, tariff and trade agreements, opening of markets to third countries, export policy, export credit measures and measures to protect trade against dumping, subsidies and the like.

As an important trading partner on a global scale, the European Union has set itself up, among others, within the World Trade Organization as a champion of liberalization. What it has achieved internally, namely the abolition of the obstacle to the free movement of persons, goods, services and capital, it is also trying to achieve at a global level. 'The world, my village' can function here as a slogan to describe politics.

To this end, it has concluded a whole series of bilateral agreements between the European Community on the one hand and countries or groups of countries on the other. By way of illustration, we refer to the Association Agreements with Canada, or to the Transatlantic Agreement with America, which was torpedoed by the Trump administration but revived by the Biden administration.

Such a process is positive and economic theories show that the liberalization of the external borders is a win–win for the participating countries. Level playing fields, as they are called, lead to greater economic efficiency, as the English economist David Ricardo already recognized in the eighteenth century. If it is easier to produce wine in Portugal and flax in England, then it is better for each country to specialize. Ricardo is therefore in favour of free trade and international trade, so that products produced elsewhere can be offered on the market at a lower price.[103]

But we must not forget that Ricardo wrote his standard work two centuries ago. It was predominantly an agricultural economy in which relocations were still non-existent. Labour migration was also rather limited. The underlying hypotheses of the model are therefore no longer

---

[103] D. Ricardo, *On the Principles of Political Economy and Taxation*, John Murray, 1817.

met. An open market in which parties do not compete with the same weapons is no longer a win–win. Anyone who conquers the European market through social dumping practices or by flouting environmental considerations is not respecting the same rules of the game.

Hence my proposal to replace the concept of a *level playing field* with the concept of a *loyal playing field*. Anyone wishing to enter the European market with goods or services is welcome as long as that country respects the same social achievements and the same environmental criteria. Such an approach is particularly required with regard to the ambition to make Europe the first CO_2-neutral continent. If all industry disappears from Europe, it will no longer pollute. Industrial policy, as discussed earlier, must go hand in hand with foreign economic policy.

In addition, it is important that Europe maintains its independence in strategic sectors. Open strategic autonomy should not be an idle word here, but lead to political action at the European level. Fortunately, COVID-19 has opened our eyes here. Europe, for all its industrial talent, was unable to produce simple masks because all relevant the production capacity had been delocalized. And the Ukraine crisis put a finger on unacceptable energy dependence.

Foreign investment and trade policy should therefore be aimed at bringing back industry (reshoring) and based on the preservation of an open market, but only for those who respect the rules of the market game. It takes political courage to impose social and environmental rules on a trading partner such as China, but that too should be possible thanks to the European Union.

One currency, one market, one vote would show citizens that the European Union has real added value. A market with 450 million inhabitants with purchasing power can, if it wishes, help determine the rules of the game. After all, a loyal playing field is a principle of fairness in which it is not necessary that every player has an equal chance to succeed, but that all players play the game according to the same rules.

Anyone who wants to come and play on the European field must therefore also respect European values. Hence my plea for a loyal playing field. For example, subsidized Chinese state-owned companies distort competition, even if they respect social and environmental rules. Europe should also show its teeth there. Or to refer to John F. Kennedy's quote: 'Foreign policy can kill us.' I would add that a bold economic foreign policy can bring enormous opportunities to Europe and its economy.

Finally, the aim is to ensure that Europe no longer depends on countries such as China and Brazil for essential products. Indeed, for more than

137 products, such as raw materials or ingredients for the pharmaceutical industry, Europe is not autonomous. In order to make Europe strategically autonomous, a strategy must be developed for each of these products, such as building up strategic stock, developing substitute products or setting up European production capacity. This open strategic autonomy should prevent the supply chain from being broken, as was the case during the COVID-19 crisis. This does not mean protectionism (hence 'open'), but a strategic, geopolitical and economic choice.

Box 12. Strategic dependency for 25 technologies

80% of the active substances used in the pharmaceutical industry are produced in China. That puts Europe in a dependent position. But Europe also depends mainly on Asian countries for many technologies. Building our own autonomy should be a priority. To illustrate, in the table below, I list 25 essential technologies in which Europe should become strategically independent. We could divide these into three categories: the first sixteen relate to digitization and production processes, the next seven to energy, and the last two to health economics.

Table 2. Strategic dependency for 25 core technologies

Digitalization and production processes		Energy	Health economy
advanced materials	cloud computing	solar voltaic energy	pharmaceuticals
advanced manufacturing	micro-electronics	offshore and onshore wind	smart health
artificial intelligence	IT for mobility	heat pumps	
augmented virtual reality	nanotechnology	renewable fuels	
big data	photonics	hydrogen smart grid	
blockchain	robotics	smart grid energy storage	
connectivity	cybersecurity	solar voltaic energy storage	
industrial biotechnology	internet of things		

Source: Compiled by the author.

CHAPTER 5
CONCLUSION

Europe needs a new narrative, a very simple and easy narrative. Just as a company has to reconsider its strategy from time to time, the same applies to Europe. Europe is neither a *deus ex machina* nor a scapegoat, but can make a real difference to European citizens in their daily life. Those citizens are the real stakeholders in the European story. A new impetus is only possible if Europe focuses on those areas where it can really make a difference for its citizens. Forget the cucumbers, the condoms and the tampons. Be pragmatic. Focus on the large, important works. We have called them the labours of Hercules.

Europe has proven that it can do so. The internal market and the euro have become feats that many envy. And yes, the process is slow. Rome was not built in a day. And yes, there have been construction errors, such as the decoupling of monetary and economic policy. But the European project has proven to be solid and able to navigate through turbulent waters and crises. Moreover, crises often appeared to act as an accelerator of the European integration process.

Crises like COVID-19 or the Ukraine conflict can also have this effect. The next-generation project is an unprecedented injection into the real economy. Financing through European loans would never have been possible without COVID-19, just like open strategic autonomy and the energy transition would never have gone so fast without the Ukraine crisis. Channelling that confidence, let us now commemorate Europe, not for its 65th anniversary, but by rethinking the role of Europe for the next decade based on the philosophy that Europe should be big in big things, small in small things. The twelve labours of Hercules can serve as a guideline here.

Let us be proud of our Europe instead of torpedoing it again and again. We are global players in Earth observation. We realized the monetary union. We have 450 million consumers with considerable purchasing power. We should not think of ourselves as the continent where the sun sets, but impose our legitimate wishes on other superpowers who are only interested in our market, but do not want to respect the environmental and social values that go with it.

Values, those are what matters. In the coming decades, values will be central. They will determine which economies have a future. America looks suspiciously at our socio-economic model, in which poverty alleviation goes hand in hand with competitiveness. China cannot survive on a one-party state where its economy only thrives under the yoke of politics and silences the politically unwilling.

If we further develop our internal market, if we align our economic policy more closely with monetary policy, if we develop a social policy worthy of the name, then the reawakened Europe can experience a reincarnation and, as far as the quality of life of citizens is concerned, become the best place in the world. And the doors for other European countries, including UK, must remain largely open.

BIBLIOGRAPHY

Aernoudt, R., *Entrepreneurship: no guts, no glory*, Intersentia, 2020.

Aernoudt, R., *Coronavirus: Electroshock voor België*, Van Gompel & Svacina, 2020.

Aernoudt, R., *Wake-Up Belgians*, Roularta Business Books, 2018.

Aernoudt, R., *Wedervaren van een Cabinettard*, Roularta, 2008.

Aernoudt, R., *Duurzaam Ondernemen in Europese context*, Garant, 2001.

Bertelsmann Stiftung, 'Estimating economic benefits of the Single Market for European countries and regions', 2019.

Birmbaum, J., *Le courage de la nuance*, Seuil, 2022.

Blanshard, A., *Hercules, een Heldenleven*, Globe, 2007.

Brugmans, H., 'Europa: ideaal van gerechtigheid', in *Europa voorbij het nulpunt*, Scriptoria, 1975.

Calligaro, M. and Cardère, E., *Les Compromis*, Payot-rivages, 2020.

Coudenhove-Kalergi, R., *Pan-Europa*, orig. 1923, Cent Mille Millards, 2019.

De Ville, F., *Winnaars en verliezers*, Pelckmans, 2018.

Derrida, J., *La différance*, Seuil, 1974.

Eppink, D.J., *Het Rijk der Kleine Koningen*, Pelckmans, 2015.

EPRS, *Mapping the cost of non-Europe*, European Parliamentary Research Service, 2014.

Gates, B., *How to Avoid a Climate Disaster*, Penguin Books, 2021.

Gerbet, P., *La construction de l'Europe*, Imprimerie nationale, 1999.

Giscard d'Estaing, V. and Smidt, H., *Europa, la Dernière chance de l'Europe*, XO, 2014.

Kok, W., 'Facing the Challenge', Report from the High-level Group, European Commission, 2005.

Lacan, J., *Les écrits*, Seuil, 1967.

Laighland, J., 'Fascisten en federalisten' ['Fascists and Federalists'] in W. Van Rooy et al., *Europa Wankelt [Europe Falters]*, Uitgeverij van Halewyck, 2012.

Levinas, E., *Gelaat*, Ambo, 1991.

Malosse, H., *Le Crépuscule des bureaucrates*, Editions Paliot, 2020.

Meadows, D.H., Meadows, D.L., Randers J. and Behrens III, W.W., *Limits to Growth, Report of the Club of Rome*, MIT, 1972.

Monnet, J., *Mémoires*, Fayard, 1976.

Office for Budget Responsibility, *Economic and Fiscal Outlook*, October 2021.

Ricardo, D., *On the Principles of Political Economy and Taxation*, John Murray, 1817.

Ruffing, F., 'J. Delors, L'homme des Firmes', in *Le fakir n°(40) février – mars* 2009.
Van der Sterren, V., 'De Verenigde Staten van Europa: een ramp', in W. Van Rooy et al, *Europa Wankelt*, Uitgeverij van Halewyck, 2012.
Van Meerhaeghe, M.A.G., *Museum of grootmacht. De identiteitscrisis van Europa*, Lannoo, 1985.
Verhofstadt, G., *De Verenigde Staten van Europa*, Houtekiet, 2005.
Von der Leyen, U., 'State of the Union', 2021.

INDEX

ABOUT THE AUTHOR

Rudy Aernoudt holds Master's degrees in Thomistic Philosophy (University of Leuven), in Industrial and Monetary Economy (University of Leuven) and in European Economy (College of Europe). He is an experienced Professor of Corporate Finance and European Policy and has outstanding international and European experience (MIT, OECD, European Commission, European Council and European Social and Economic Committee). Uniquely, he has occupied Chief of Staff positions at European, national and regional level and served in the Belgian government as Secretary-General for Economy, Science and Innovation. He is currently Senior Economist at the European Commission dealing with space economics, enterprise and entrepreneurship, financing of enterprises and industrial policy, and Professor of Corporate Finance at the Universities of Ghent and Nancy and at the executive Master's of BMI.

Milton Keynes UK
Ingram Content Group UK Ltd.
UKHW021619100424
440940UK00022B/281

9 781839 703225